Advan

The Life That Woke Me Up Was My Own is a book of remarkable depth and transformation. I was swept up in, and moved, by Nancy's beautiful descriptions of nature and by her journey toward healing, consciousness and joy. As we are let in on Nancy's profound inner journey, we are also taken on a trip within ourselves. This is a book that is meant to be read by our heart and soul, which then allows our mind to heal along with Nancy's.

Margaret Paul, PhD, Co-creator of Inner Bonding® and author of *Healing Your Aloneness; Inner Bonding; Do I Have To Give Up Me To Be Loved By You?* and *Do I Have To Give Up Me To Be Loved By God?*

Nancy Swisher's honest, compassionate, and compelling explorations of her silences and truths allow us to attend to our own. Through startling images of nature, as much as through sharing the movements of her exploring mind, she encourages us to wake up to what we may be avoiding and to trust our own spirit. If you want to know more about who you are and have always been and can fully be, read this book.

Judith Gold Stitzel, PhD, Professor of English, Founding Director of the Center for Women's and Gender Studies at West Virginia University, and author of *Field Notes from Grief: The First Year*

This is the touching story of an old Soul who remembers and forgets — and eventually remembers again — who she really is. Written with clarity and poignancy, it draws the reader into the story of a person who experiences great loss and gains strength, love and much wisdom in her lifetime. This book will inspire you to more fully engage with your own journey of transformation and conscious evolution.

Robert J. Brumet, M.S., Faculty, Spiritual Development and Pastoral Studies Unity Institute and Seminary, and author of *Finding Yourself in Transition; The Quest for Wholeness; Birthing a Greater Reality: a Guide for Conscious Evolution* and *Living Originally: Ten Spiritual Practices to Transform Your Life*

The Life That Woke Me Up Was My Own is an inspiring and thought-provoking combination of storytelling and spiritual wisdom. Through her own stories of loss and growth, spanning from childhood into her later years, Nancy reveals how our experiences both shape and trap us in limited versions of who we really are. She then shows us the keys that release us from our own stories to live a more fulfilling and authentic life. This book reads like a captivating heroine's journey while providing insightful guidance for how to heal from our own past loss and trauma.

Megan Walrod, M.A., Founder of Live Your Yes, LLC, Transformational Business Coach and co-author of *The Energy of Healing*

This book blew my mind! I stayed in the same position the whole of yesterday afternoon and read it from cover to cover. When I finished, I wanted to read the next one. It was healing in the sense that it brought me home to myself. I want all my clients and guests to have a copy. I can't think of one person that I wouldn't highly recommend this book to.

Fran Stockley, Founder of BodyLove Luxury Detox Retreats

Nancy Swisher's *The Life That Woke Me Up Was My Own* is a must read for any woman who has looked at her own past and has seen a very special child whose voice became silent. Her story unfolds in the most eloquent writing style and sometimes reads like a novel, but it is truly a memoir of how she transforms her life to align with her own spiritual awakening and steps into her authentic work in the world as not only a highly skilled writer, but also as a healer and spiritual mentor. Through her story, Nancy reminds us all that no matter how difficult our life may seem, when we are able to view it from a place of awareness, it indeed supports us to become who we are meant to be.

Kaya Singer, Author of *Wiser and Wilder: A Soulful Path for Visionary Women Entrepreneurs*

Some books, like *The Life That Woke Me Up Was My Own*, transform us through their depth and authenticity. Nancy Swisher's lyrical narrative paints a dynamic portrait of a rich and complete life. I was reminded of Anne Morrow Lindbergh in the way Nancy expresses her connection to nature, to her spiritual beliefs and values, and to her precious canine companion, Horton. This memoir shows a life path that is both remarkable and splendidly ordinary, both profoundly spiritual and deeply rooted in the physical world.

This beautiful book gives us just one example of what a life looks like when it is "filled with the consciousness of Being," and it inspires readers to look at how they can participate more fully in the creation of their own unique lives.

Amy Waterman Mason, Parent, educator, poet, and author of *Lessons in Letting Go*

Nancy Swisher's memoir offers a wonderful example of how self-love and consciousness can blossom in the midst of — and often as a result of — our painful life experiences. I am grateful for Nancy's willingness to write not only as a gifted and talented sculptor of words, but also as a vulnerable, authentic human being to whom I can relate.

Karen Kral, M.A., LPC, CoreQuest Counseling & Retreats

Reading Nancy's book awakened a voice within me that had been dormant for many years. I was then inspired to write my truth and express it in the world.

Sandra Swan, Career Coach for Midlife Professionals

Nancy's memoir wraps around you like a finely-woven tapestry of spiritual wisdom and insight: the chronicle of a life lived and witnessed from the wisest part of our collective Self. She takes us on her journey of knowing her deep Self, first losing the connection with Self, and then finding it. She inspires us all to lead a more conscious, gracious life.

Mike Moran, Certified Inner Bonding Facilitator, Certified EFT Couples Therapist, AASECT Certified Sex Therapist

THE LIFE THAT WOKE ME UP
WAS MY OWN

A memoir

Nancy Swisher

Thomas Noble Books
Wilmington, DE
www.thomasnoblebooks.com
ISBN: 978-1-945586-00-2
Library of Congress Control Number: 2016944218
Printed in the United States of America
First Printing 2016
Cover design by 2FacedDesign.com
Cover Art: Nancy Swisher
Editing by Lois Rose

Arrange whatever pieces come your way.

> ~ Virginia Woolf

The great central fact of human experience is the coming into the conscious, vital realization of our oneness with this infinite life, and the opening of ourselves fully to the divine inflow.

> ~ Ralph Waldo Emerson

You need to claim the events of your life to make yourself yours.

> ~ Anne Wilson Schaef

Dedication

This book is dedicated to my clients.

And to Mom, Dad, Tom, and Horton.
I feel your love from the other side every day.

Contents

Introduction

I've called this book a memoir. Memoir is a form, a literary form, created by literary minds. The first time I studied writing at the Women's Writer's Center I confronted my battle with form. Each student, except for me, knew what form her writing was. She knew whether she wrote a short story, poem, or novel. (At the time, literary memoir wasn't taught.) I, on the other hand, said that I wrote paragraphs. So when the state of New York decided they would no longer award poets and prose writers the individual artist grants in the same year, but that they would alternate, and the year I was there would be poetry, I simply made line breaks on my paragraphs, not changing one word, and I won one of the grants. That was 1983.

What I learned from this experience validated my knowing that it is my Essence, when I align with it, that transmits wisdom and inspiration in my language, not the contrived form that another person says is the correct one. It was the consciousness behind my words that influenced the judges. Making line breaks didn't change that.

Just as it doesn't matter whether the words I wrote were poems or paragraphs, it is not the external form that matters, but the consciousness of a person. But we live in a world of form as well as a world of Spirit. The tricky part is that from a very young age, we are conditioned to separate from our knowing that we are beings of consciousness, or Spirit. We learn that our body and mind *are* who we are. Most people around us are lost in thoughts and survival modes of behavior. We must learn to survive our environment also, and so become disconnected from the deep knowing of our own Soul.

The Life That Woke Me Up Was My Own is about my journey of having known at a very early age that I am a spiritual Being, but getting lost and disconnected from that knowing. This book shows the choices I made that reconnected me to my original knowing. Each of our lives is meant to do this in a unique way.

It is my hope that all of you who read my book will be transformed by it, that you will begin to see how your life has unfolded perfectly for your own reawakening. Although this book is not a typical self-help book, but a *literary exploration of personal growth and transformation*, I believe in the power of personal narrative to transform when it is filled with the consciousness of Being. It's simply more intimate. And that's a good thing.

A Reader's Companion Resource Page

I encourage you to read this book first for the pure enjoyment of the story, the language, and the heart and soul experience it offers. Then, I suggest you use the Resource page on my website to go deeper with your own journey of finding your voice and exploring your own awakening.

On this page you will find:

- A set of 20 inquiry questions to guide you toward your inner wisdom and the voice of your deepest Self. These are perfect for book groups.
- A self-discovery assessment tool on the subject of Find Your Voice | Stand Behind It | Change the World.
- A guided audio meditation for tapping into the Presence of love within you.
- A Facebook Study Group

Go to this link to access your Resource Page:
http://nancyswisher.com/bookresources

1.

Mom's Death

I was born June 23, 1951, in Keyser, West Virginia. I was born again on April 9, 1959 in New Creek, West Virginia, located five miles south of Keyser. The first birth was when I came out of my mom's womb, took my first breath. The second birth was the day she died.

The day Mom died, I was sitting in my second-grade classroom at my small wooden desk. My friend Jimmy sat behind me and had just handed me a penny Tootsie Roll. Our fingers tickled each other's when Mrs. Harris, our teacher, looked to the back of the room. The school secretary, Martha Martin, had opened the door and motioned for her to come back.

The two of them stood in the back of the room at the door whispering to each other.

Then, Mrs. Harris walked over to my desk. "Martha needs you to go with her," she said. "Let's get your things."

I closed my arithmetic book, slid it into my satchel. Mrs. Harris took my green and red plaid coat from the coat rack for me to put on. I felt on stage.

I walked across this stage to Martha, standing in the open door holding out her pale white hand for me.

"Say something," I wanted to shout. But my words remained asleep and motionless behind the tight place below my ribs.

In this silence, we walked the hallway to the school kitchen. To our left, Cecil Dawson, the janitor, spread sawdust on the wood floors to absorb oils and dirt before he swept. It wasn't the regular kind of dry woody sawdust like Dad used on the meat market floor, but a green, granular institutional product that smelled of chemicals. Cecil bent at the waist in his charcoal-gray work clothes, throwing the stuff like birdseed.

To our right, the sixth-grade door stood open. All the kids' faces turned to look at Martha and me. My sister Sally's seat was empty.

We entered the narrower hallway that led to the kitchen, which was empty except for Sally, who stood in front of the deep, stainless steel sinks, looking out the window at our house on the hill up from the school.

The bright, spring sun made our brick home appear clean and perfect. Dad walked from the front door to the carport. Then stopped to look down at the school. Could he see us peering out the window? I could almost see the bricks clearly enough to count them. Almost. The way you can see some stars, the Pleiades, for instance, out the corner of your eye but not straight on. The bricks were like that.

Mrs. Thomas, the school cook, came into the kitchen carrying five racks of Bumper Bread. She placed them on the counter with a sigh, turned to Sally and me, "Let me give you girls a hug."

Memory stops here.

Then picks up again when Dad pulls into the carport, turns off the engine of his light green Buick.

The three of us get out of the car and huddle like teammates, looking down at our feet as Dad begins to speak. "Your mother passed away this morning," he said.

I knew he said 'passed away' instead of 'died' because it seemed less painful. I knew what he was feeling. Our silence the moment he stopped speaking felt like the opposite of a miracle, like the Red Sea closing in. I looked up and saw two crows. The sun made their black feathers look blue as they flew over our house and out of sight.

Inside, Janet Fike, our neighbor, and Aunt Kathleen, Dad's brother's wife, waited to comfort Sally and me. I sat on Janet's lap, pushed my face into her shoulder. She held me but didn't speak. She smelled like homemade bread. I cried and thought about never seeing my mother again, except dead in the casket. And that would not be her. My mother herself was gone from this moment on. Her death became a story.

* * *

Days before the funeral, I could still see Mom at Markwood's Funeral Home on Main Street. We went at least once a day. Standing in the dark velvety room with the casket, I couldn't stop staring at her face. I had never seen a dead person. The blankness drew me in — the powder, lipstick, and rouge — all with nothing behind it. Where was she? Where did her breath go? I imagined she might wake up. I had seen this happen in a movie. I thought I saw the tiny wrinkles of her closed lips move.

No more smile.

I heard whispers of "poor girls without a mother" throughout the crowded parlor. "That's me," I thought, "they're talking about me."

* * *

My father bought a blanket of a hundred red roses for Mom's casket. He said they symbolized his love for her. He held my hand tightly as we sat in the fourth pew from the front, listening to our Methodist preacher narrate my mother's life. I cried, and I stared at the roses. When I wasn't staring at the roses, I looked at the large painting of Jesus on the wall behind the pulpit. He stands with two lambs, holding the smaller one in his right arm, the larger one on the ground looking up. He wears a wine-colored robe that drapes. The sky behind him resembles the sky outside our living room picture windows. Long, blue mountain ranges on either side. Magenta sunsets. Green valleys where sheep graze. There is a golden halo around his head. My favorite place in the painting is where the smaller lamb's belly rests on Jesus' arm. I imagine that this is where love enters the soft belly of the younger lamb.

When I looked at the painting during Mom's funeral, I felt love in my belly too.

I had no words for my experience; I had no one to talk to about death, or love, or the smaller lamb. Without words, days and months and years tried to cover over my new awareness that the love I imagined in the painting was also within me. I didn't know as a child, or as a teen, or as a young adult, that I didn't have to fear forgetting the presence of Divine Love, that it was always available, that it was the Essence of me. It would take me a while to remember.

* * *

It snowed the day of the funeral. The weight of the snow caused the spring forsythia to touch the ground.

Cars followed the hearse up the Queens Point Cemetery hill where cinders had been scattered for traction.

The grave had been dug ahead of time. Standing at its edge I thought about yesterday, imagined men digging with shovels, tossing dirt into the sky as the snow began to fall.

The preacher read from the Bible. We sang a hymn. The wind howled and whipped our faces.

Mother was definitely gone. I couldn't hold onto that fact the way I wanted to. I needed to know where she went and how long she would be there. I needed Dad to tell me.

He never talked about death. But at the funeral, and afterwards, I fantasized he knew what I was feeling as a motherless child. In my fantasy he understood every single feeling I had; he talked to me about grief and loneliness, told me not to be afraid. In my fantasy he understood the snow on the forsythia and why I had to place myself there and how the beauty of nature helped me feel grounded on Earth.

* * *

We had fried ham for dinner. I asked for the piece with the round ham bone. Then sucked on the bone. The salt of its crispy marrow sank into my heart and kept me company.

* * *

Awake at night, I tried to imagine how long she would be dead. Remembering the stars in the huge night sky above our house, I figured she would be dead the amount of time equal to how far away the stars were. So I traveled in my imagination to the brightest star, but just before I arrived, a click in my brain brought me back to my room with its brown-flowered curtains and orange bedspread, which in the dark, faded to nothing.

Each night afterward I pushed further, making a game out of finally reaching infinity. If I could do that, maybe she would be there waiting. But I never managed to get there and eventually stopped trying.

Looking Behind Me

My mother's early death trained me to live in my memory. I thought by turning my perception behind me, I could keep the memory of her close. I thought that if I remembered the pink peonies we cut for her headstone every Memorial Day, that if I remembered the smell of the air as the turkey buzzards circled above the cemetery, that if I remembered the words my father spoke about how much he loved her, I could remember her. But what I kept close to me was not Mom, but the absence of her, along with the feeling of sadness, which for years I confused with love.

If my life is a boat going down a river, my past the wake, and my present-moment me standing at the front watching the boat part the water, I ask, "Is it possible to be in the moment while having my head turned backwards?" It's all a metaphor, actually, but as I live life, as I learn to be more completely in the moment, body, mind and Spirit aligned between earth and sky — at times I still turn and look backwards. Inevitably, every time I do this, my heart leaps out into that sad place that took root so long ago.

Being Looked For

1956

My favorite game in the summers of my childhood was hide-and-seek. I especially took delight in hiding. My house was in the country so there were many sheds, garages, all sorts of bushes, large trees, and odd places to hide, like under a porch or under a house. If it was dusk, which, in my opinion, is the best time to play, the sounds of the whippoorwills saying goodnight, the sparkle of the lightning bugs finding a mate added to the magic of hiding, the magic of being looked for.

When whoever was IT yelled out, "Ready or not, here I come!" I felt such excitement. My whole body tingled. I thought I could burst out of my skin holding back sheer joy. But it was more than a children's game for me.

I longed to be found. Not literally, not as part of the game. I wanted to win, to run to home base before I got caught. But there was a different kind of being found that I sensed. I wanted to be found in the sense of being seen, understood, and connected to. As we say now, "I wanted to be gotten."

At a very young age, shortly after birth I suppose, I was aware of the absence of connection among people, although I had people around me. I had a father who loved me. A mother who loved me. And a sister who loved me. Still, I perceived a disconnection, an empty space where words should be, where gazes should be, where touch and holding should be. So playing hide-and-seek, hearing someone say, "I know you're out there somewhere," offered me a moment of feeling the excitement of being found.

Freedom

2008

Synchronicity is how the Universe creates itself. There is no time. But my training is to write as if there is time. To tell a story as a story. This happened, then this happened, then this happened. I have never been comfortable with that structure, though I've tried to squeeze myself into it, writing for teachers, writing for journals, writing from a place of thinking about what someone else would *think* of what I write. The tiniest speck of this kind of perspective, however, removes me from the language I am searching for. *This* language. *This* way of putting sentences together. And I do love sentences. And words. And how words, when you speak them aloud, over and over until they create a vibration inside your body, until there is a resonance between your Spirit and the words, make life shift and change and open up doors to lit rooms awaiting your entrance into the next desire of your Being.

Just the other day I talked with a friend who is still a friend. In '75 she met me at Oxford, where I had gone to study Shakespeare for the summer. We then traveled through Europe for six weeks. Ten years after that, I moved into the ashram where she lived. In our recent conversation, more than twenty years after the ashram, we spoke of our Europe trip and we were inside that time period — we were experiencing the freedom of life in this moment as we spoke of the freedom of life we had then, our commitment to be free, to live free, to not become trapped inside jobs and marriages and standards of behavior made up by others.

As we spoke, me in Iowa City, she in the Berkshires, I felt the truth of no time. We had expanded beyond our day-to-day lives of paper, dinner, sun and moon. I was exhilarated. I retrieved a piece of myself I left back there when freedom was not just a word but a lifestyle, not just a lifestyle but a determination to always seek the feeling.

"I already am who I want to be."

When I was five years old, the milkman at my father's store asked me a very important question, which I didn't realize at the time was a very important question. It was a Saturday morning. The very bright summer sun had just come over our mountain. I was playing hopscotch on the sidewalk in front of our store next to our house. In 1956, hardly any traffic passed on the road in front of the store. In fact, most of the time it was so quiet that I could hear the creek across the road, the slightest breeze, the crows, woodpeckers and sparrows. I loved this kind of silence.

The milkman drove to our small grocery in New Creek, West Virginia from Cumberland, Maryland. We were just five miles from the state border. He was the tallest of all the deliverymen. On this morning, as usual, he stacked the milk cartons onto the dolly to wheel them inside. But just before he opened the front door of the store, he paused, looked down at me, and asked, "What do you want to be when you grow up?"

I raised my hand to shade my eyes as I peered up at the tall man. Without an ounce of hesitation I said, "I already am who I want to be."

I don't remember what happened next. I could speculate, which I will do.

The milkman may have told my father what I said. I may have gone into the store for a Popsicle and overheard them laughing. But what I do know is that the milkman ignored my answer.

There was just one question, one answer and no follow-up, which of course is just the way it was.

However, because there was no follow-up, I noticed something quite new beginning to occur. A little void took root, a little cave where my words inhaled, withdrew, and learned to love the darkness more than the light.

When I said, "I already am who I want to be," I had spoken what I would call, much later in my life, my soul words — words that come straight from my heart, where our deepest truth lives. I knew I was Spirit. I knew I was a Being of consciousness. But I needed someone else to know this with me.

When there was no follow-up, given I was only five, my human self quickly made a decision. Was I wrong for saying what I said? Is that why the milkman said nothing? Was that a crazy comment?

And so, a thought passed across my brain. Perhaps not fully conscious, but there nonetheless. As time passed, as more and more of my soul words garnered no response, the thought about being crazy repeated itself. It must be so, I thought. Why else would people act as if I had not spoken?

My past began to take root with this false self-concept. I say false because I was not strange or crazy or wrong, yet in that void of silence, my human self began to doubt.

Home

2008 Iowa City

Horton, my dog, a black Lab shepherd mix, is presently the love of my life. As we walk past the Catholic church on this sunny morning before the service begins, the people walking toward the church all look at Horton. A woman with a huge smile approaches, barely looking at me, holds out her hand to pet Horton's large black head, exclaiming, "I love dogs, I love dogs."

We continue through the neighborhood, past the red bee balm, the orange daylilies, down the grassy hill to City Park. As we approach the first pond, I hear the killdeer squawking. I smile. The killdeer brings my father's spirit to me. I know this because I feel it to be true. I was happy before I heard the bird but then my happiness expanded. "Hi Dad," I say. (Horton sniffs the grass.) Dad's been much more present for me since he passed over than he could ever be on this plane. When I was younger I told him to make sure he connected with me after he died so that I would know there was an afterlife. He sure is keeping his promise.

"Finish the book!" Dad says through the sounds of the bird. He cheers me on, which is what he tried to do in real life, but there were some glitches, there was some wreckage.

Healing

The root of the word 'heal' is the same as the root of the word 'whole'. When most people think of healing, they think that there is something to be fixed within them. There is nothing to fix, only a true perspective of Self to find, only wholeness of Self to feel. Believing untrue things about oneself causes all of the emotional pain we typically seek to remedy. Healing is the process of becoming conscious of these unconscious beliefs and the painful feelings they cause. Thought precedes feeling. Most of the time, people are not conscious of the thoughts that cause their feelings, but slip into the feeling unconsciously. I liken thoughts to slippery fish. Until we catch them, grab hold of one, examine it and ultimately choose it or not, we are not living a conscious life.

2.

Crazy

In the summer of 1961, my father, sister Sally and I drove across the West Virginia hills toward our house after picking Sally up from her 4-H Camp, which was situated along the Potomac River in Romney. It was dark. We were quiet. The hills were quiet. Out of the blue, Dad started talking to us about a *Reader's Digest* article he had just read that day about how smoking causes lung cancer.

"I don't want you girls smoking," he said. "Cigarettes discolor your skin, make you smell. You've seen the smokers who come into the store, like Virgie Cosner. No man will ever want to be with a woman who smokes."

Dad hated cigarettes, though he kept a crumpled pack of Salems in the drawer of his nightstand. (He smoked one occasionally if he played cards after his Lion's Club meeting.) The article scared him, perhaps because it was written from the point of view of "Joe's lung", which made the description more real.

His rant moved to the subject of death, wherein he proclaimed that there is nothing after we die.

I must have been feeling quite brave and full of myself in that moment, for I piped up, "It will be just like before we were born. It won't be nothing." When I heard my own words I felt like a string of colored lights, filled with certainty and knowing that tingled my ten-year-old body. I continued, "It will be peaceful and warm with hundreds of new colors."

"You're crazy," Sally snapped from the back seat, then cackled with laughter.

"Nancy, don't you think that's a bit far-fetched?" Dad added.

I had no idea how to explain my knowing. In fact, it felt impossible. All I knew was that the words I spoke about what it will be like after we die came from a place inside me that felt infinite, that matched the very thing I was talking about. Eternity.

In my silence, Dad began to sing "Beautiful Dreamer", his favorite song for harmonizing on car trips. But Sally interrupted him.

"You are crazy," she shouted louder than before.

"Be nice to your sister," Dad said.

"She is," Sally said.

As they argued about my state of mind, I disappeared into my throat where my words dissolved into white blood cells preparing to fight the sore throat I would awaken with the next day. "Maybe I am crazy," those cells thought.

They Didn't Mean To

2008

Even though I just wrote about a memory of being told I was crazy and believing that I was, I am presently feeling rather blissful, for I am now clear to the bone that whether or not I feel a particular feeling is my *choice*. I am clear that any pain I feel in my present life from this incident is caused by me, attaching to the old self-concept created during the drive home.

When I was just a small girl, I didn't know about such a choice. I wasn't aware of my thoughts as thoughts. I didn't realize that I was attaching to a thought when I felt the shame. In my child experience, I identified with it. In my child experience, I *was* it. Thus, my soul words were silenced. I silenced them. I protected them.

To write about such an experience is tricky because I must focus on the dark drive home as if I am experiencing the dark drive home.

So I turn my head to the maple leaves outside my window. "I wish the red ones would stay forever."

In this moment, of being with the red leaves, they are there forever.

The Ship Metaphor

I practice thinking of my life as a ship on a river. I am the ship and the river. I am the physical — the ship; and the nonphysical — the river; I am the particle, the ship; the wave, the river.

Today, I felt as though my ship were disconnected from the river, run ashore on dry land. Stuck. Rather than feel the pleasure of anticipating pages not yet written, I focused on the fact that they weren't yet written. Rather than imagine the joy of creation, I judged its absence. I was caught in the human habit of focusing on what one does not want, rather than imagining what one does want.

In such a predicament, my choices are to 1) judge myself for feeling stuck and out of the water; 2) keep doing *something* to shift my energy and create a little relief (meditation, visualization, various forms of energy alignment and release techniques); 3) eat; 4) become frightened at my state of non-productivity by comparing myself with other, more productive people, such as Oprah; 5) worry about whether or not I am supposed to write the book at all; 6) call my homeopath, thinking if only I had a remedy; 7) do breath work; 8) call a friend; 9) rest; 10) trust the flow of my energy even though it feels like it's not flowing at all.

I picked #10 and found myself in the TV room watching the video of my Uncle Arnet's home movies from the '50s and early '60s. Soon, I am transported into the world of my childhood — snowstorms in the Allegheny Mountains, birthday parties, Christmas dinners, my cousin and me at The Enchanted Forest, my mother smiling just months before she died. I am seven. I watch as if I have amnesia and I'm trying to identify a person I should recognize, studying that child who was me. My hair is cut short and uneven like a mistake. Soon, I feel me at age seven, my sense of being different, odd, not like my cousin or my sister.

Do I judge myself for watching this? No, I do not, even though I had been reading *The Power of Now* a bit earlier in the day, which could have fueled such judgment, for here I was, being with the child I was just months prior to my mother's death. I chose this 'now'.

Later, at the dog park, I speak aloud to myself while Horton eats grass along the fence.

"So what have I been thinking or focusing on today that made me feel like that lost, abandoned little girl that I was?" Answer: "I've been focusing on absence: the absence of in-person friends; the absence of more written pages; the absence of new art on my walls." I realize that I had been focusing, though quite unconsciously, on lack rather than Presence.

As Horton and I continue our walk, I begin to consciously choose thoughts that feel much better, like "I always learn from my days", and "Things always get better", and "I needed to see how I am still creating the feelings of that child I was so that I don't do that anymore!" That one feels real good. So I shift my mind, thus my feelings, thus my entire vibration.

I'm flowing again, ship and river, body and Spirit, rising to a feeling of peace.

"Horton, let's find a four-leaf clover," I shout to him across the park. I scan the clover for no more than fifteen seconds. (I have no doubt.) There it is, staring back at me, a perfect little four-leaf. I pick it. The little lost girl whose mom died so long ago wants to cry at my manifestation because she confused sadness with love. But I say, "No, child! Tears are not for this. This is a moment of Joy! We can be joyful right now and always."

Horton walks over to see the clover.

A Great Horned Owl calls from the woods beyond the park. I look up.

History

I own my history as historical. When I see my life as a ship, my history is the trail I leave behind. From a certain human and psychological perspective, the trail has a huge impact upon my subconscious beliefs, which hold the vibration of all the programming that is not fully conscious. I write about that history here, not as truth, not as who I am, but as a piece of the puzzle along the way of realizing the reality of me. I am an individualized expression of God. I don't mind using the word God. I mean Divine Love when I use the word. I mean Mother-Father God. I mean I am a point of consciousness within Infinite Mind.

Eagle Power

2008

The eagles are back. They have been gone for the summer months because the heat in Iowa is too much. I've been anticipating their arrival for weeks. I love the eagles and want to be with them in the sky. I stare up at them with longing on days when my mind thinks thoughts of doubt, as if their power and beauty is something far away from me. But on days when my mind, body and Spirit are lined up, I fly with them; I hear their messages. Today, their message was "Trust your words."

I can lose sight of the Eagle Power if I am not disciplined in my thinking, for it is thought that creates. The two eagles that fly above me clearly inform me to move to another level in my power to create by taking charge of my thoughts — by not allowing programmed thinking to enter, not for one minute, one second. Can you imagine hearing this from an eagle? I am so happy to receive this message today, for today is the day I needed to receive it.

I have not written for days, and a small bit of doubt had crept into my body, causing me to feel heavy like bread that refuses to rise.

Doubt is quite ridiculous. I am happy to finally know this. But, as with all things new, the excitement in the moment is momentary, and therefore lost if I try to hold onto the feeling. Thank you, Eagle.

3.

The Sixth-Grade Essay
Incident

Success 1962

She was the sixth-grade editor of the small school paper and her teacher encouraged her to enter the state history essay contest. Her father, a self-proclaimed historian, insisted on helping. Her topic, the father said, would be John Brown's raid on Harpers Ferry. He was a Civil War enthusiast, proud that West Virginia became a state during the war, siding with the North, separating from the South, from Virginia.

After the family dinner, he and she would go to her room to work on the essay.

She watched his strong, thick hands, more familiar to her than her own, finger the pages of library books searching for relevant details about the raid. "Put this in your own words," he said. He handed her a passage describing the U.S. Arsenal.

"What's an arsenal?" she asked.

"I'm surprised at you," he said. "Weapons are made and stored in an arsenal. Write the description of the town, how the arsenal was situated on the hillside overlooking the Shenandoah where it meets the Potomac."

Her thoughts drifted. She thought about the year the raid happened, 1859. Then she realized the raid was exactly one hundred years before her mother died. She asked her father if she could put that in somewhere.

"You never put anything about your own life into an essay," he said.

* * *

Fame

A photographer from the town paper comes to her country school to take a picture of her, which will accompany the small article in the next day's paper — "Local Wins State Essay Contest". She wears a brown corduroy jumper her stepmother made, white knee socks, and a white blouse. As the school principal hands her the Daughter of the American Revolution medal for her winning essay, the girl smiles. The flashbulb pops. Then, the principal says, "We are so proud of you, you are very lucky to have a father who cares about your academic achievement." For a split second, the girl feels numb, as if she were two-dimensional instead of three, a flat paper doll whose jumper hangs by folded paper tabs. Luckily, her mind comes to her rescue, directs her thoughts to the memory of the cinnamon toast she ate for breakfast.

After school, her older sister waits at the foot of the hill by the cherry tree outside the school kitchen.

"You're such a fake," she yells. "You know Dad wrote the whole thing."

"He did not."

"He did too. Everyone's laughing at you. I told them he wrote it."

"They're not laughing."

"You're so naïve," says the older sister.

"What do you mean?" says the little sister.

No sooner had her words made sound than the sky began to swirl. Vertigo engulfed her. The yellow goldfinches flying about the hayfield became a blur. She focused on her breath, the color yellow, and then closed her eyes.

* * *

The photograph appeared in the *Daily Tribune* the next day. The day after that she received a clipping tucked inside a congratulatory card from the editor of the paper. She kept this card and clipping for thirty years, until the day she finally remembered all of what had happened during those evenings writing the essay.

Writing About Forgotten Experience

Use of the third person to describe the young sixth-grader as 'she' rather than first person 'me' is of course intentional. The 'I' of the 'she' didn't recall anything out of the ordinary during those evenings working with Dad. I won. This was my first success in the world according to the world. Dad sat too close. He touched my leg. He looked at me the way he was supposed to look at my stepmother. Although I could feel how this was not supposed to be happening, I was inarticulate. I was eleven.

My body remembered but these memories weren't conscious. My emotional and sexual self withdrew from my mental and spiritual self. This split made sure that whatever it was that happened during those essay hours would never happen again. And it didn't. If I locked away those parts of myself, I could have control. So I shut down all conscious connection to my budding sexual energy. Along with that, of course, I disconnected from my innate feminine power.

This sort of split is, at the very least, disempowering. But more than that, for me, the voices in my head created still more stories to make sense of it all, more false self-concepts, more feelings of shame that would silence the fullness of my wisdom and spirit and power for a few decades.

Through the Lens of Vibration

I must speak about vibration more directly before moving on. We carry a vibration with us from one part of life to the next, whether it be the next decade, the next marriage, the next job. And what creates our vibration? Primarily, our self-concepts, both the conscious and the subconscious ones. We carry the thoughts and feelings of our conditioned, our programmed, mind away from the father's house, into the world. For some, that world occurs in the same zip code, a short journey. For others, the world is the university, or the military, or a marriage. This vibration or frequency determines a large part of how our life unfolds.

For instance, the belief about myself that I accepted on the drive home from 4-H Camp that I was crazy created a vibration of self-doubt. I doubted my ideas. I doubted my perceptions. This belief colored my world. It helped to form the lens through which I saw things. It seemed true and it seemed real. Not all of me but a part of me felt crazy when I had a brilliant idea. So I kept them to myself for a long time.

A Fraction of Myself

I left home in the fall of '69. Had someone asked me how I was, I would have said, "Fine," which I was. I would have said I had the best father anyone could imagine, which I did. I would have said I was against the Vietnam War, which I was. I would have said all of this in a soft whisper, however, for I could speak only a fraction of myself. I did not know why, for the why existed in my subconscious. I believed my faintness of voice was my true self. I believed the feelings of being different belonged to me because they *were* me. Therefore, I carried into my new adventure not an expressed excitement about forward motion into the world, not an exhale, but an inhale, a held breath, a withdrawal from the world, as if to say, "I'm here but I want to go back." And I did go back. I returned to my father's house most weekends, to walk in the woods, to work in the store, to be with what felt familiar. Going back meant returning to what I knew to be me. I knew myself in relation to Dad. I knew myself in relation to the self I created during those first eighteen years. I was that. I was a daughter.

It's a law of quantum physics that what we focus on expands. So why not focus on all the wonderful aspects of the first eighteen years of my life? The flowers, the canoe rides down the Potomac with Dad, the fun times with customers in the store, family dinners. Why focus on the unremembered?

Here's the reason: in order to ascend into more Light, the wounds must be made conscious. The straw cannot be ignored when spinning the gold. You can't release something you are not conscious of. The traumas and events that cause the false self to form in the first place must be acknowledged in order to gain the wisdom of knowing oneself. Integration. Making the darkness Light.

The Oriental Lily

2008

I buy an oriental lily the week before New Year's to place in the bud vase on my coffee table. It's magenta and white with three buds. One blossom has come and gone. The second opened New Year's Eve while I slept. It is in full bloom now. The third is puffed out and ready to open. I want to see it open. I think of staying on the couch to watch until it opens. I would fast from everything but staring at the lily. I go out instead.

I drive along the Iowa River while listening to Eckhart Tolle talk about the pain-body. Just when I understand his teaching yet again, I look out my window toward the river, and flying low about eye level is a bald eagle. I decide to go to the dog park to see more eagles. Horton senses my decision and begins making excited dog-noises.

He and I arrive at the park. On this day, the temperature is in the thirties, which is warm for January in Iowa. The sun is bright and the geese are swarming again and again. You would have thought it was spring, hearing them honk and scatter with their powerful goose energy.

On this day, it's the geese that get my attention rather than the eagles. A flock of geese heads towards the river. I ask them to come back and fly over me. They turn and come back so that I can look up at their beautiful bodies, feel their love and begin my day with the magic we are here to experience.

Belief: what we know to be true in our mind coupled with what we feel to be true in our heart. Beliefs are the language that speaks to the quantum field. Among the birds, I experience this clearly.

4.

The Summer of '71

This was the summer the *New York Times* began to publish the Pentagon Papers. This was the summer Nixon signed the bill to lower the voting age to eighteen. This was the summer Jim Morrison, the lead singer of The Doors, was found dead in a bathtub in Paris. This was the summer Gloria Steinem delivered her "Address to the Women of America". In the midst of what was then called the 'Cultural Revolution', this was also the summer I wrote in a journal for the very first time.

I had traveled with Janice, my best friend from high school, to work for the summer in Hyannis, Massachusetts. Janice and I first met because she had read the write-up about me in the local paper when I won the sixth-grade essay contest. She looked forward to my arrival at the high school from my country school. She said she knew we would be friends because I was smart too, like her.

I was excited to live by the sea and to be far enough away from West Virginia that I could feel the larger world, beyond the pull of my father and my father's land, the millions of trees, the ceaseless Appalachian hills, their special power that taught me how to love the Earth and, in so many ways, made me happy to be alive. I longed for a new experience of myself.

Janice brought Hermann Hesse books with her that summer, which she shared with me. She also brought a journal. I watched her write each morning as the sunlight streamed through our window. I wanted to be like her, to have her confidence, though what I really wanted was to be me, to be my own confident self.

Janice's mom taught high school English. The student she talked about most is now famous. Henry Louis Gates. She called him Skip. She always said he would be famous. He made her classes come alive, she said. Janice's mom was also the first adult woman I felt seen by. It was such a new experience that at times I would sit across from her in her living room feeling simply ecstatic, thinking "This is how human connection feels." She looked at me as we spoke. We paused between exchanges. I had never experienced communication like this in my family.

Janice passed some of the mothering she received on to me through the kindness and understanding of a best friend.

"You should keep a journal, too," she said one morning as we drank our Lipton tea.

So I bought a yellow spiral notebook with lined paper. Alone in our room one morning, I made a decision to write. I felt an odd sensation, as if I had reached for a journal just like this a million times before. But I hadn't. I lifted the notebook from my nightstand. I watched as if I were in a movie, only this movie was directed by me, by my heart, and though I had no words to describe or understand this moment as it unfolded, I remember it now, some thirty years later, because it was the moment the life I'm living now began. It was the moment I began to give voice to my Spirit.

I chose the pen rather than the pencil.

I wrote without thinking.

I wrote words about Being itself:

> Alive, finding out one reality.
> Grasping it, releasing it.
> Alive, each moment aware of more.
> Looking inward. Never comparing.
> Alive, standing alone.
> Within. Waiting for myself.
> Burst. Human Being.

With each word I wrote, my body shifted from feeling like rock to feeling like water. The words belonged to me. They weren't my father's words or words to please my father. My sister would not see these words to call them fake. I had connected to language, expressed my Self through language, recognized an ancient respect for language, and allowed my heart to open to language.

Those words seem so simple to me now, so contained and timid, so constricted, so abstract. But they were the beginning seeds of my private expression, which would be my primary lifeline to wholeness, back to the Being I knew so well that morning playing hopscotch on the sidewalk in front of Dad's store when the milkman asked his question.

Uncertainty

When I write, I am required to sit here, many times uncertain where to go next. Not that I don't know the story. I do. But the context for the story has to do not only with the time-space dimension I live in, but with the eternal part of my Being also. With what I call the horizontal axis and the vertical axis.

The challenge of embracing true uncertainty is trust. What do I trust? What does trust feel like? What if I have parts of me who don't trust?

I trust God, All That Is, the quantum field, the part of God that I am, and my participation within this Universal field of energy. Trust feels like emptying my mind, momentarily, and listening for another voice, other than the ones already programmed. Trust feels like fully embodying my physical form with an attitude of love and awareness. When I wrote in the yellow notebook I was totally uncertain. I didn't know what I was going to write. I was just twenty years old. You could say that being uncertain is the same as being aligned with Essence. That's how I define it anyway. And when I'm aligned with Essence, I may be uncertain in the sense of not being able to think ahead, explain, or figure out; however, I am quite certain of the feeling of alignment with Source. I didn't have all these distinctions and experiences to draw from in 1971.

My uncertainty now is no different than my uncertainty then. But I'm different. There's more of me. That's because life unfolds me. Or I unfold life. There's an evolution. A conscious evolution in my case because that's all I ever wanted. That's all I ever longed for: to know the truth about my Spirit and my human self and how they mix and how they inform each other.

Desire

I use the word 'desire' for the first time. I use it in connection to my Spirit. Spirit is in a constant state of expansion. Our individual Spirit has the blueprint for our desires, which you may call purpose (though purpose changes and grows over a lifetime). Think of it this way: the caterpillar desires to become the butterfly; the acorn the oak tree.

When leaving the family of origin, moving out of the house, going to college, getting a job, whatever the human being does when they leave, the choice is either directed by true desire or false desire; from a deep place within or from a role society deems responsible; from Essence or conditioning; from God tapping on our heart or the need for approval in order to feel worthy.

I had no desire other than to leave. Even that was a tiny desire. I knew I would go to the university. I knew I would stay in the dorm with my best friend Janice as my roommate. I graduated thirteenth in my high school class so I knew I would pass my courses. The kind of knowing I experienced at eighteen came from my conditioned mind almost entirely though. I didn't know how to go within and ask my Spirit what to do. I couldn't feel truth. I had no body awareness to speak of. In fact, my body felt like it was wrapped in Saran Wrap, holding me together, hiding a secret I could not name, or touch, or connect my conscious awareness to.

We All Do Have a Story

2008

If we don't have a story, we don't have to live up to it. I understand the wisdom of this statement. Yet there are moments when I want to shout out loud, *"But damn it we all do have a story."* When I feel like this, I know that I am stuck inside the story, feeling limited, constricted by circumstances, and at the effect of the world.

I take Horton to the dog park.

I see eagles. They sit motionless on the black branches of the huge pin oaks lining the banks of the Iowa River. Some look down upon the river searching for fish. Others look toward the park. Occasionally, they fly overhead. I walk to the part of the park closest to them. I stand still. I stare into the distance where they sit. I ask for Guidance. I beg. I do this only on 'those days' — the days when I feel so utterly disconnected from God, from my Self. Those days I'm identified with my story. As I stand there talking to them, I begin to laugh at myself. The eagles help me to remember that I always have a choice over being conscious of my thoughts. Suffering lies in refusing to choose. So I choose.

5.

English Composition Class

I'm a freshman at the university. My in-class English composition receives a D. My take-home composition on the My Lai Massacre, wherein I argue that the responsibility for the atrocity was upon the top military officials, not just Lieut. Calley, receives an A. Due to this discrepancy, my teacher calls me in to her office to ask me if I had indeed written the Vietnam essay, since my in-class one, where I was told to describe a vase she had placed in front of the room, received a D.

"How could this be?" she asked. I didn't know what to say. I had written both. I couldn't write about a vase. I could write about the war.

"There's a place inside me, (I could not say this) where the words come from. When I feel no passion, there are no words. I can't fake the words, (I didn't say)."

I did not say, "I can't write when someone is watching me." My body remembered Dad sitting beside me at my desk in front of the mirror, writing my sixth-grade essay, but my mind had no memory whatsoever. My body remembered. But these words, which I now use so freely to describe what I felt then, I did not feel then, because you can't really feel without being conscious of the feeling. I was not conscious. Since I had no conscious awareness of my body and its feelings, these words were far away from me in 1970. The thoughts I unconsciously believed about myself, the thoughts I accepted from Dad, Sally, teachers, the world, all of which informed me that something was deeply wrong with me, began to rise up, into my inner world, as a self-concept based in shame. The body that remembered everything sat in my teacher's office basically mute, although I said I wrote it, which I did.

When I wrote the My Lai essay, I felt clarity within me, where I knew what my truth was — that the war was a display of insanity, that Calley was part of it. When I looked at the *Time Magazine* photographs of the massacre, words poured forth from my heart with the suddenness of the white-tailed deer when I surprise them in the woods. But my teacher questioned their honesty. She questioned whether the words were mine. She did not believe me. Her judgment felt familiar. Yet I was not conscious of why, but simply felt afraid of her.

Inner Space vs. External World

If I had had words to describe to the English teacher why I could not write a descriptive essay about a vase, while I could write an argumentative essay about My Lai, then my sense of self, or self-concept, would have felt more solid to me. I could have felt a *me*. And this me wouldn't have been about opinions or status or intelligence, but simply a me that I could feel and give words to.

I would have said to the teacher that the vase had no meaning for me and that I didn't know how to give it meaning. To write four pages about it, as we were assigned, seemed like a lie and that this is why the writing received a D. It was lifeless. It was devoid of Spirit coming through me.

Had these words been available to me then (of course the consciousness would have had to have been there too!), my entire life journey for the following three decades would have unfolded differently. I can't begin to imagine. But the words and the consciousness of Self were not available.

The English Teacher and the
Lens of Vibration

There's another aspect to the English teacher incident in terms of looking at how the first years, when the conditioned mind forms, create the years that follow right after leaving home when we 'live out' the beliefs we carry.

My conditioned mind, which formed from events such as the ones in my life I wrote about here — 'Mom's Death', 'Crazy', and the 'Sixth-grade Essay' — is made up of beliefs about myself and the world along with the feeling states or vibrational frequencies of those beliefs and self-concepts. I was not walking around my college campus consciously thinking, "I am a fake" or "Something bad is going to happen," yet I carried most definitely the vibration of those beliefs.

In turn, I attracted to me experiences, the scary English teacher, people who would reflect back to me the fear itself, providing proof that there was something quite real in the world to be afraid of and something quite innately wrong with me.

Did I understand how I attracted the teacher? Of course not. I do now though. And the magic of clarity, no matter when it occurs, is that it transcends space and time, so that I can take a seat beside the eighteen-year-old me, struggling to write about a vase that had no meaning to her and reassure her that she is brilliant, beautiful, and whole.

Tundra Swans

2008

Horton excitedly jumps out of the car. The sky is filled with formations of pink clouds that swirl like the taffy we pulled in the church basement when I was a child. I stare at the clouds for a moment, fascinated by how they look. I love how different geographical areas have unique cloud formations. (The clouds in Iowa are amazingly beautiful.) The air is clear because of the storms that went through earlier, bringing autumn temperatures. As I stare at the clouds, suddenly I notice, to their left and much higher in the sky, a migration of tundra swans flying south.

Even though they are very high, their whiteness is incredibly bright because the setting sun shines directly on them. Upon seeing the swans, I know immediately that they are the reason I have come to the dog park this evening.

The power of the tundra swans on their journey home feels like a shot of truth flooding my body, a connection to a power much greater than me, much greater than any of the mundane worries I carry with me this day. I feel connected again to the part of me who understands I am Spirit, who understands how their migratory path is innate just as my homing mechanism to be my essential Self is innate.

They reminded me that I choose my thoughts, for once I saw their beauty I could no longer allow any negative thoughts into my mind. The worry dissipated instantly.

Later that night, when I awakened at 3:00 a.m. and the little worry thoughts tried to intrude again, I had my tundra swans to focus on. I made a choice.

6.

The Date

In 1973, my junior year of undergraduate school, I rented my first apartment with Janice. Our apartment was one of four in an old, run-down, typical college rental — on Stewart Street in Morgantown, West Virginia. I was a biology major, enrolled in organic chemistry, animal physiology, and physics. Janice was an English major. She shared her reading lists with me. That year I began to consider changing my major to English because the memorization required in the sciences had the effect of separating me from my Spirit, although I did not have the words for this feeling at the time.

That fall, my biology lab partner was a guy named Ben. It turned out that his apartment was just down the hill from ours. Occasionally, walking up Stewart Street from the main campus, I would stop at Ben's to visit: drop off lecture notes or study sheets — something like that. Always welcoming and kind, he would offer European cookies and tea. Ben's parents were from Holland but now lived in Texas. Sometimes when I visited, Ben would play a newly composed song on his guitar. As I listened, I would find myself imagining that I was his girlfriend, lying next to him beneath the skylight, on his India print bedspread where magenta elephants marched towards the Ganges.

But outside my daydream, I couldn't find the girlfriend part of me. I tried. I smiled at Ben in biology lab, then forced myself not to avert my eyes when he smiled back. A challenging task it was.

For the biology lab final, we were required to know the entire anatomy of the cats we had been given to dissect at the beginning of the semester. I invited Ben to my place to study. He brought his cat and we sat at my kitchen table, our cats spread open in front of us. We memorized muscles, tested each other. We labeled the organs, the kidneys, the tiny heart. I made tea for him. He wanted to play me a song he had written that day. He said I had inspired it.

I had already decided I could never be his girlfriend. "It would never work," I told myself. By doing this, my impossible-to-find girlfriend self could keep her feelings hidden away.

When Ben played his new song, all I could think about was whether I was listening correctly. My utter self-consciousness blocked me from receiving his song. In this state of protection, I began to compare myself to him. He was a tall, Dutch blonde who played guitar. My home was just two hours across the West Virginia mountains. Ben's talents were still alive. I stopped playing piano and flute at fourteen. His walls were decorated with insects he'd caught in Madagascar, then mounted and framed; original pencil drawings matted and hung; photographs from Holland. I had only mass-produced anti-war posters.

"I need to keep studying," I said. "I really don't know these muscles yet." This was my response to his song. He looked disappointed. I made another cup of tea.

We took our exam on a Friday, and Saturday afternoon I sat in my apartment reading Wordsworth. It was a glorious October afternoon with red leaves swirling in the wind, blowing across the sidewalk outside.

"Our birth is but a sleep and a forgetting." "Our birth is but a sleep and a forgetting." I recognized these words. I knew they were true, so I read them over and over until my understanding absorbed them as mine.

As I repeated these words, I saw Ben's silhouette through the white chiffon curtain panel on the front door. Ben knocked. Quickly, I ran from the couch to the tiny bathroom where Wordsworth fell from my hand into the claw-foot tub.

Ben's knocking persisted. I hadn't planned to hide like this. Running from the couch in the living room to the bathroom was a reflex based solely on the suspicion that he wanted to ask me out. Once hidden in the bathroom, however, my mind kicked in: If I went out, we would eventually have sex.

I heard him call my name. I felt like I was in a movie with hundreds of people watching me. I was the sympathetic, but disturbed, protagonist. It would be impossible for her to answer the door. The story of why had not yet been written. The man who wanted to date her would give up, walk back down Stewart Street to his apartment, play guitar. He would find another more normal girl.

I stared at my face in the mirror. Did Ben know I was home? Could he see me standing here? Did he hear my breath? These thoughts felt devastatingly shameful. Worse, I knew that I could do nothing else. I believed something at my very core was bad, that my twenty-two-year-old body housed a room with a dirt floor. Without knowing who the demon was, I tried to stare down shame itself.

Shame is a complex entity, much too evasive for a twenty-two-year-old to pin down. Was my true nature only available to me when reading literature that inspired me? Could I feel whole and completely real only when facing a book, not people? I yearned to feel natural, as it seemed Janice usually did, flirting and fun-loving but still smart and empowered. She would have gladly dated Ben had he ever asked her, which he eventually did, and they went off to Mexico to collect butterflies the following summer.

Shame won that day when Ben knocked on my door.

Ben finally left.

Wordsworth stayed behind in the tub while I steamed an artichoke, melted butter, and dipped each leaf, then scraped it with my teeth. I stared out the kitchen window. The neighbor's children played in the colored leaves raked into a mound, orange, yellow, scarlet, screaming as they belly-flopped into the pile. The heart of the artichoke was my favorite part. I cut it into small pieces, chewed each one slowly.

Healing Shame

Sometimes shame occurs in the area of money, sometimes in the area of relationships, many times for women in relation to their body or intelligence. In 'The Date', I attempt to describe how shame felt to my twenty-two-year-old self. At that point in my life, I didn't have the word shame, or the consciousness about what I was feeling.

Feelings occur in the body. At twenty-two, I did not feel my body or see my body with full awareness. You could say that I was not embodied. I lived in a state of dissociation from my body.

If I had had consciousness about feeling shame, I would have been able to connect the feeling back to the thought that created it. From there, I would have been able to see the experience from which I created the thought. Such connections define consciousness. The thought would be something like "I am bad." And then, once isolating the thought or belief about myself that caused the shame, I would have connected to my Spirit, my Being, the non-physical part of me, and asked if indeed this belief were true. But I'm way ahead of myself.

Shame caused me to hide; that is its nature.

The me who read Wordsworth and listened to the leaves, the me who recognized my Being — the transcendent part of my Self — for a brief moment while reading "Our birth is but a sleep and a forgetting," over and over aloud to myself, that me, suddenly jumped from a moment of peace to a moment of fear, hiding from a good friend who I believed wanted to go out on a date with me. I did not understand my own behavior. In fact, I used my behavior as evidence that there *was* something wrong with me. This is how the patterns of the conditioned mind work, whether it be trauma or simply a belief programmed by society, such as "Everyone gets the flu at some point." (The programming being that the flu is caught! That we do not have any part in whether we get the flu or not.)

Needless to say, these two examples are not equal, in that believing you are going to get the flu wouldn't cause a fearful response, a hiding response, though it would create getting sick.

A child's forgotten trauma, however, whether it be overwhelming feelings of abandonment after a divorce, physical violence or simply neglect, creates a ripple effect in life, on the horizontal plane, causing actions that make no sense (my jumping off the couch), yet feel impossible to stop.

I could always return to Wordsworth though. His words, "Our birth is but a sleep and a forgetting," awakened me to my Self, to the eternal part of me. His words were a portal to the eternal Being I knew I was. I would find more words that carried upon them the meaning of the Universe, providing me an external reference through which to find my Self.

Still Spinning the Straw

2008

Occasionally, still, the programmed thoughts, the story and painful feelings that are my false self take hold of me, try to turn me in the other direction, away from joy and freedom and light, into the darkness of false beliefs and the fear that stops me in place, like a fly caught in a spider web.

For a moment, I feel crazy. For a moment, I believe that if I am successful, something bad will happen, like when I won the essay contest. For a moment I believe I am a fake.

I suppose it is inevitable that such moments occur as I write about the journey of becoming free of identifying with these thoughts. I don't mind.

I have the opportunity to choose to shift my focus to the truth of my Being, to the reality of me. It is this choice that creates the gold.

7.

Women's Studies

1975

My copy of Tillie Olsen's *Silences* is old now, with yellowed pages and thin tears across its spine. I first read the chapter 'One in Twelve: Writers Who are Women in Our Century' in my undergraduate women's studies course the year I switched majors from biology to English. I underlined this passage:

> How much it takes to become a writer. Bent (far more common than we assume), circumstances, time, development of craft — but beyond that: how much conviction as to the importance of what one has to say, one's right to say it. And the will, the measureless store of belief in oneself to be able to come to, cleave to, find the form for one's own life comprehensions. Difficult for any male not born into a class that breeds such confidence. Almost impossible for a girl, a woman.

I drew on Olsen's theories to try to understand my silence, the way it had lasted for years, and seemed part of my body's chemistry. I read and reread, consuming her words like medicine, hoping for a cure.

I felt less alone, knowing other writers experienced silences as well, yet on a deeper level of private thought, I still felt different, as though my particular version of silence was not named in the book. Still, I tried to blot out that knowing. I tried to let this book explain my silence to me. "Yes! This is why my voice hides, why I can never quite say what I think, and feel anxious around most people. It's all because I was born in Appalachia to a father with a grocery store instead of a law firm. Born female. Middle class. These are the reasons."

The problem with Tillie Olsen's premise, however, was that other women in my women's studies course, who, like myself, were Appalachian and not rich, weren't silent at all.

There was the very talkative Irene with her odd combination of long hippie skirts and perfect make-up. She voiced her opinions so freely that sometimes it was like she was teaching the class. And Joanne Miller had already published poems. When she entered the room everyone looked up at her beauty, knowing she would go on to study at the best post-graduate program.

I remained confused about my silence. Rather than speak up, which would have been the feminist thing to do, I pretended to be fine. I didn't know where to put my confusion. After all, it was literature we were discussing, not our fears but the fears of characters in books. At this point in my transformational journey, confusion served me well; it shielded me from memories I was not yet able to allow into my consciousness.

My women's studies teacher was Judith Stitzel from Manhattan. She came to the English department with a reputation for being a great teacher, a feminist, student-oriented as opposed to academically driven. I had never met a woman like her. I loved just looking at her. She seemed happy and energetic, excited about her ideas. She had ideas! "Why do we want what we want, and don't want what we don't want?" she asked one day. Could I allow my mind to join her in this inquiry? How excited I became at the promise of the possibility. However, sitting silent at my desk, rather than tapping into my wants and desires, I felt blank.

Judith's voice was vibrantly loud and her laugh long. She liked herself and wasn't ashamed. She wore glasses with large tortoise-shell frames and her brown hair was cut short. Her clothes showed the shape of her body, colorful large print fitted blouses tucked into tapered pants with a belt at her small waist. Her style reflected her own pleasure with how she looked. In fact, Judith's example of physicality was itself a feminist model — she defined her looks, not Madison Avenue — her body was not cut off from her ideas.

When she sat on her desk discussing Olsen's point that one out of twelve writers is a woman, her arms moved like fluttering birds, marking her passion for conveying this knowledge to us. She must have been born with a kind of bravery not available to people like me. I reasoned it must be city strength. Yet, these thoughts were not fully conscious. Not then. In my silence, where the Being that I was felt smothered by feelings I could not fully connect to, I sat peering out toward this teacher and the others in the class, from the perspective of isolation.

Still, I could tell by the way Judith looked at me that she knew I had ideas too. She stared me in the eye, smiled with embrace, as if waiting for my thoughts to materialize, wrapped up like presents in spectacular language. She believed that a teacher's expectations did indeed create the students' achievement, or at least had a great impact on it.

I didn't want to fail her. But I was helpless in my fear of making my thoughts public.

The talkative students frequently stayed after class to speak further with Judith about a book or an issue. I always walked by them, pretending to myself not to care if I was part of their group. But their laughter and their loud certain voices followed me into the dark hallway where I disappeared into the crowd of students. I couldn't block them out. I made this moment a snapshot of my identity.

No way could I be like them. Yet, sometimes I imagined that Judith would ask me about my silence, perhaps sit with me in her kitchen, someplace private, where lilies or hydrangeas were perfectly arranged. There, a word, a touch, a sudden connection between us might prick my memory and lead me into a lighted world, where I would be able to respond like the women in long skirts, normal and free, without fear of repercussion or judgment.

But Judith had no idea I needed her like this. In my world of silences, I would fail her. I couldn't rise to her expectations. "I am so much more than I am able to express," I longed to say, "so much more than I appear to be."

Although I could not share publicly my private thoughts and contemplations, the intellectual stimulation of my women's studies class — Tillie Olsen, Judith's personality and wisdom — inspired me to begin journal writing. In fact, the day I cowered on the inside while walking past the group hovered around Judith after class, I walked straight home to my attic apartment and wrote.

Nov. '75 Working towards preciseness through variation — to say exactly the circumstances of some aspect of daily life, to say precisely with words what is real through time and space, layers and layers of details must be piled upon one minute of consciousness in order to surround it and reveal it by those surroundings. It is the objects which are real, it is the kitchens, and the bruises and the touch of skin, the shrubs with tiny red berries that you pass sometimes if you walk a certain path through campus, the same path that has the patch of sky that catches the sunset and jet stream, which is always there at sunset, the only thing you know for sure. How to get at your preciseness — you must first recognize the details — you must laugh at the people and cry and shiver at the deadness of the animals on the highway and know the hardness of a particular asphalt step and what you saw and heard and felt and thought at the moment of recognition about that hardness — the associations, the layers, the connections and the patterns past and to come which make that moment a precise one in the memory.

The clarity and peace I felt as I wrote in my journal I didn't feel in the world of people. There was a split. These words had to be private. I did not think this was unusual; I did not question why my private words contained so much more freedom, so much more spirit, than my public ones. All I knew was that my most important reality was inside my journal.

The Journal and Judith

I was in my early twenties when I took Judith's class. I had just changed majors from biology to English. Only by looking back do I see how her class opened me to an inner world that had, up to this point in my life, remained walled off, mute, numb. The combination of someone like Judith, along with the books we read, and the other women's voices, provided the contrast necessary for me to realize that I must find my own voice, that I was not willing to live in silence.

There was the yellow spiral notebook from Cape Cod in '71, but other than that one writing event, I had not written consistently from a place of knowing that language connected me to my Essence, my Spirit. I had not felt the utter pleasure of that until I began to keep my journal. So even though I couldn't express myself in class, I could and did express myself when I wrote in my journal.

The journal became essential to my life. This was not a coincidence, but a direct result of being in the presence of someone who seemed to me to be quite fully expressed as a human being. And hers was a public expression. I could not sit in class without being affected. Judith's spirit dusted me with particles of Light that landed and went home with me, where their alchemy began, nudging my own words onto the page, words that caused me to feel real and alive upon reading them back to myself. A private magic was born.

Language, my own language, the voice which came

,rough in those first journals of the early '70s, became the touchstone that would guide me through periods of my life that followed college, until finally, I connected to the words I lost as a child, the ones that just wouldn't come out of my mouth in Dad's presence, or in Sally's presence, or even in the privacy of my own room, with the orange bedspread, where I played Janis Joplin, pretending to be her.

And this was exactly the way it was all supposed to happen. Part of me knew this also. Knew that Judith and I had a soul connection, that our souls would serve a purpose in each other's lives.

One day I would be able to see the perfection of how my life unfolded, but only after I ceased to believe that there was something deeply wrong with me. And this would take years.

Why Years?

I could say, "Because it did." This is true. But I ask 'why' and I like to answer. Many people look back on their lives and say, "If only I hadn't married him," or "If only I had known that would happen." The underlying assumption being that something is wrong with how their life has unfolded.

I prefer to see my life as unfolding perfectly. Actually, it's not so much a preference as a knowing that it does. "The place you are right now, God circled on a map for you," said the poet Hafiz. And Rilke: "Life is always right."

I have experienced those 'if only' moments, however. I have said, "If I had known in my twenties what I know now, I could have produced so much more work." There are countless incidents I could look at. My clients do. I then attempt to inspire them to reframe their story, for it is a story, it is a narrative that we live within. And it is our choice to create a narrative that empowers or one that does not.

Devoted to the Unfolding

2008

The prairie winds blow 50-mph gusts. After the toughest Iowa winter in almost a century, spring is here. The sun is very bright; the turkey buzzards fly high, and the fat robins peck for worms. Horton and I are the only ones at the dog park. As we walk, I ask, "Is the physical part of me (my thoughts, feelings and actions) a vibrational match to the larger nonphysical part of me?" I ask the question because simply by asking I know I'll receive the answer — not immediately, but after three circles around the park, after the killdeer tells me to protect my creative projects, after the cardinal chirps and chirps to remind me of my feminine power, I hear, "Yes, you are aligned."

My mind and body have been acting out lately, dwelling upon such thoughts as "I can't write this book," "The book is crazy," "It's not your purpose," "Something bad will happen if you complete the book." I do not want to empower these negative thoughts by focusing upon them.

They do surface however! Then I get to choose where I will focus.

The real me is happy and joyful and loves to write. The real me explodes with laughter 'at the drop of a hat'. The real me smiles, imagining exploding with laughter.

I am devoted to the unfolding of my ability to *be* the real me. I am devoted to the process. I love flowers because they are a bud, then a full bloom, then they die.

The process of spinning straw into gold is like the flower. Today's straw, those pesky thoughts about this book, held in consciousness by my eleven-year-old who made them up — they are the straw that becomes the gold. But the transformation does not happen without intention, without consciousness, without caring how I feel.

I write from the present because I don't want to pretend that I have no more straw to spin. There's very little of it, I must say, but it surfaces, primarily in the form of thoughts. When I can bring the Presence of my true Self to the painful feelings the thoughts create, then all is well. The birds help me.

I could not live without the birds. Simply knowing the eagles are gone until next winter, I feel part of me is gone also.

Segue

My unfolding continued when I decided to go to graduate school for my master's in English. It was *King Lear* that drew me in. I loved the play. My Shakespeare teacher was offering a semester graduate seminar on *King Lear*. We would read it line by line. It was that one seminar that had me decide on graduate school. While there, I developed an interest in teaching composition as well. I wrote my master's thesis on the work of the French structuralists. Judith was my thesis committee chairperson. I had a graduate assistantship to teach English. Dad paid for me to go to Oxford to study Shakespeare in the summer and to travel for six weeks around Europe. I had many good things in my life..

8.

The South

1978

The night before I left Morgantown for South Carolina to begin my first teaching job at Voorhees College, one of the historically black colleges in the U.S., I dreamed about Jesse Jackson. He was walking across a large, bright green lawn. The green was overwhelming, iridescent, amazingly beautiful; I couldn't take my eyes off it. The atmosphere of the entire dream had a green glow. Jesse's mother was ill. He wanted to reach her and he was rushing, his black shoes tapping down the wet grass quickly. Pecan trees formed a canopy, creating dappled sunlight. I watched him. I wanted to meet him. I felt a sense of spiritual home when I looked at his face, like sitting in church as a child staring at the stained-glass windows. Or sitting under the red oak tree on the land next to our land in autumn. Places I felt safe. A double rainbow appeared above Jesse and the pecan trees. His mother sat on the edge of a car seat with the door wide open, waving to him. She wore white cotton gloves, a pink Sunday church hat and a flowered dress.

When I walked into the classroom at Voorhees and saw my students, I had the same feeling of spiritual home as in the dream. I called roll: Queen Ester Hicks. Roosevelt Caldwell. Ambrose Scott. Idella Green. Diane Cleveland. Lakeisha Perry. Dill Littlefield. Hercules Brown. The dream of Jesse, his mother, the rainbows and green wet grass resided in my heart right then. The students' kind faces, their acceptance of me and mine of them, created what seemed like an immediate bond between us. They began to ask me about my life, where I came from, if I was married. My openness gained their trust. Soon in the semester, we would discuss stereotypes on television, racism, sexism, and classism. The female students confessed that they watched soap operas, but said they knew how stupid they were.

Queen Ester wore a hat that first day of class. She sat in the front row, avoided eye contact, but smiled when she thought I wasn't looking. Roosevelt teased me about my color, and refused to take off his hat. The administration required no hats in class, but I ignored the rule. Lakeisha said she wanted to be a writer. Idella said when she was a little girl a friend of hers was lynched. "You don't believe me, do you," she said. "Of course I believe you," I said.

We discussed white Standard English, how it was necessary to learn if they wanted good jobs. We looked at endings like 's' and 'ed' and how to correctly use them with verbs. They taught me their dialect. Hercules wrote an essay about shallow graves, turtles and cypress trees and said that he didn't believe he could ever get a job better than manager of Kmart. "That's not true," I said.

"Maybe for you it's not," he said. "My brother graduated from here and that's where he ended up. Over in Orangeburg managing the Kmart." I didn't argue with Hercules. How could I say for sure what kinds of opportunities he would have? I wanted more than anything to inspire and give hope to the students, but I was white, and therefore my word, no matter how much conviction lay behind it, came from my experience in the white world. That's all I had. Yet, I felt so similar deep inside. I, too, had always felt a sense of alienation in the world.

Every Friday afternoon was assembly. The student gospel choir wore royal blue satin robes and guest speakers stood behind the podium of the auditorium stage. Tony Brown in March, Julian Bond in April. Jesse came in May. The chairs were outside that day, arranged in semicircles with an aisle up the middle, all under the shade of the water oak trees. While Jesse spoke I closed my eyes and remembered the dream. This was the green lawn. These people, my new home. Jesse ended his speech that day by encouraging everyone to stay off drugs and affirm themselves by chanting I AM SOMEBODY I AM SOMEBODY I AM SOMEBODY. We all shouted together. I saw Queen Ester start to cry. And Idella. Even Hercules.

I cried too. A spiritual uplifting happened among us all.

Our energies synchronized; our intentions merged into one. We aligned with the words "I am somebody" — words which pushed out the tears that belonged to another belief, the false belief, the misguided belief, and the programmed belief all of us shared: that something is terribly wrong with us.

On the Monday following that assembly, Queen Ester asked me why she had to write the way I was teaching her. "What's wrong with my natural voice?" she asked.

"Nothing," I said. "It's beautiful."

But if I gave her an A for her real voice, the administration would reprimand me for not insisting the students learn how to write white Standard English.

The judgment required of me felt wrong. Yet, I wanted them all to succeed. On nights when I graded their papers — marking grammatical mistakes, confusing sentence structure, and spelling errors — I questioned whether what I was doing was destructive. Was I helping to mute their true voice? Was I telling them that who they were in their essence wasn't good enough? I feared this. I didn't want to participate in taking away anyone's voice.

When none of my students received any grade lower than a C for the semester, the academic dean, Dr. Marla Jenkins, called me in for a meeting. "Ms. Swisher," she said, "I'm disturbed by this." She pointed to my grade sheet for the semester. I said nothing. She was a large woman who hardly ever smiled. Her reputation was one of severity, commitment to the school, to standards. I had seen her speak with contempt for the students who 'acted up'.

"I know Benjamin Jones could not have earned a B. I can't have you giving grades to our students when they don't earn them. That's what teachers have done all through school. Don't you understand that?" Her suit was magenta that day. The jacket had large gold buttons about to come undone with each breath. I felt frightened and mute. "Don't just sit there, Ms. Swisher," she said.

"I tried to grade fairly, Dr. Jenkins," I said.

"Fairly, Ms. Swisher, would look like a distribution of grades which includes D's and F's." She shuffled papers on her desk. Paper-clipped my grade sheet to a piece of pink paper that looked official.

"I taught them how to write, Dr. Jenkins. I taught them invention, not grammar. They learned to generate language. They learned to love writing." My words wouldn't stop. For a moment, I didn't care what she thought of me. "I encouraged them to observe the things around them — whether it be city dumps, pink plastic flowers, eye contact with other people or trees — to discover their own preferences, their own relationship to these things. I taught them to find their writing voice."

"We don't pay you to teach that, Ms. Swisher. We pay you to teach them to pass the standardized tests. We are a poor institution, Ms. Swisher. If they don't score on those tests, we don't get grant money. If you don't conform to the way we do things here, I'm afraid you won't be rehired."

"I understand," I said.

Contrasting Experiences

The dean was right. I wasn't doing my job. This particular student was at the bottom of the class. But because I cared so much for him, I couldn't fail him. Because I truly loved the language of his speaking voice, the meaning it carried, I couldn't give him the grade I should have on his written papers. I knew that if I failed Benjamin, it would cause him to feel more shame than he already felt. I couldn't do that. You see, when he and I talked, face-to-face, there was no shame, not for him or for me. When we talked, our spirits connected; we had fun; we laughed. The part of me that truly believed his language deserved an 'A' in the world of grades understood more clearly than the part of me trying to teach Standard English that I would not last in the academic world. I wasn't a teacher; I was a healer, a counselor, a person concerned with the Soul; a person more comfortable with the invisible world than the visible. Thus, correcting verb tenses and plural endings would soon become unbearable.

The South gave me my first big lesson in contrast. By contrast, I mean I began to realize what I did not want, which, in turn, began to stir within me imaginings of what I did want. By contrast, I mean that as I moved through the five-sensory world, I simultaneously began to allow my Inner Guidance to come through, to direct me toward my deeper desires, to the situations and people that supported my highest good, my purpose. For instance, when called on the carpet by Dean Jenkins, did I walk away feeling that my beliefs were nuts? Yes. Or did I walk away judging her? This too. How could I find a higher ground than either of these options? I didn't have the spiritual understanding to do this. My seeking occurred just under the surface of my conscious mind. When I had to make a big choice, like whether to sign a contract for another year, I struggled to trust myself.

I was alone. My connection with the students buffered the aloneness, as did the cypress trees, the peach orchards, and the cows grazing. I had left my home state, my family, and my friends from graduate school. This is what one does. But without the inner connection to my Self, which I didn't know was not there, moving out into the 9-to-5 world like this felt not only meaningless, but also rather frightening. Why didn't I choose a more mainstream profession? Why did I end up at Voorhees, one of the poorest colleges in the U.S.? Questions like these I didn't ask then. I can look back now and ask them, but I know the answer. I attracted Voorhees in order to get the experience of spiritual connection with a group of people; in order to see the effects of racism in America; in order to learn about nuclear waste (the largest waste dump on the East Coast was just thirty miles from campus); and most importantly, in order to realize that I did not belong there, that I could not grow there because I was not, at my core, a teacher but a healer. The contrast allowed me to feel my life direction more clearly.

I returned, for my second and last year there, immersing myself in the contrast once again, until I awakened enough to choose a new direction.

Guidance

1980

The summer between teaching contracts, before my last year at Voorhees, I had my first-ever astrological reading. Mary lived on a farm outside the small West Virginia town where I was staying that summer to study theatrical clowning. She was the first astrologer I had ever met.

I did not want to go back to my job in the fall. I knew this because when I imagined going back I felt fear. However, I didn't know what else to do or how to figure out what to do. Without my teaching job, I would have no income. Perhaps Mary could help.

She introduced me to her cats and I felt immediately at home. I had given her my birth information on the phone, but now she had me press my palms into ink to read my hands. I loved the ritual.

After sitting in silence, except for the loud cardinal just outside her window, Mary began her reading. The first words out of her mouth were: *Did your father abuse you?* The word 'abuse' was new to me. In college, my housemate helped start the first shelter for battered women. Other than words in conversations with her, abuse never surfaced.

I smiled. "Oh no," I said. "He was domineering but he never abused me." I was certain of this. Though she accepted my response without question, I felt a door had opened. The word caused a quiet reverberation in my body, like a sound that has moved far beyond hearing distance.

My biggest fear in 1980 was nuclear weapons and the possibility of a nuclear meltdown worse than Three Mile Island. Mary told me to trust the Earth. She said the Earth is much more powerful than all of the men upon it. She also told me that I was not part of the 9-to-5 crowd, that I was part of the New Age and that this frightened me because my sister and father were very much part of the old order. She said I was an esoteric counselor, not a teacher. At twenty-nine, much of this felt very true but making it real in my life wasn't yet in my skill set.

Mary's presence acted like a magnet to bring forth more of my own Presence. Indeed, it was a turning point. Although I did not suddenly, magically, manifest a new job or a new direction, I had touched a place inside which would grow and transform forever.

9.

My Intuition is Born

1981

I stayed at Dad's house the week before I drove back to South Carolina for my last year of teaching at Voorhees. I slept late each day. My joints ached. I had headaches. Dad came back to my room one morning and said, "You can live here if you don't want to go back down there. I'll support you. You can write." His words felt wrong, wrong like a mutation is wrong. They felt bad and slimy like I had to protect myself from them. I tensed my muscles, tightened my stomach. I felt a small round pain the size of an olive just beneath my left ribs.

"I could never live here," I said with judgment, pushing back at him, wanting my words to hurt him.

"Suit yourself," he said. "But stop complaining."

He was right. I should be grateful. It was my own fault I felt lost and unable to hook into life, the way normal people did. I thought of Janice, who already had a job at EPA. She told me she'd stay there for her entire career, get retirement, that sort of thing. I felt like an astronaut on a spacewalk, floating in the deep black universe, hooked to the world of people and things by only a small thin cord. My cord was Dad, his money, his house, the land. But if I went back to Voorhees for a second year, I could at least keep searching for another kind of connection to the world. Maybe I'd feel more part of the place this time, be a better teacher. I did not realize the connection I needed was a connection with myself, my Essence.

* * *

At the first faculty meeting of the semester, I met Ken. He had been newly hired to teach remedial reading in the Learning Resources Lab where I taught writing. He was tall, blonde, red-faced, and drove a very old antique car. He was from North Carolina and had taught college for a few years.

By the middle of the school year, Ken and I rented an old southern farmhouse, with thirty-foot magnolias framing the front porch. The house sat amid pastureland, where brown and white cows grazed all day. For a short time, I basked in the feeling of normalcy that I thought I wanted: I was teaching college, I had a boyfriend, and we lived together. The externals were there at last. Looking at my life through the eyes of my father, through the eyes of society, I was succeeding. But through my own eyes, which continued to turn more deeply inward toward my Spirit, I eventually had to admit that the daffodils sitting in the sunlight on our kitchen table brought me more joy than anything Ken could possibly do or say. I did not understand why this was, but I knew it was true. I could feel the truth.

Jan. '81

I believe within the nerves of my intelligence that if I don't keep alive my interiors, if I don't make space for my own nurturance, that if I stop constantly to include the person I love, then my creativity will cease. My strength will dissipate. And my life will be empty and I will be like the other women I see, who would rather lose their interiors than lose the love of a man. I refuse to do this. I refuse to reach that point. I will never say that I'm painting my living room when someone asks me about my work.

It's morning. There's a bluish fog outside where the cows graze and the kitten plays. I have to teach in twenty minutes. I dreamed all night a feeling of restlessness with my life, a need to move, to create more order, more peace. I must remember that I am not trapped, that my choices are not self-destructive. There's no time to write now.

* * *

During spring semester, I researched places to study writing the following year. Ken supported this, though we both knew he would stay in the South.

March '81

Ken and I make love after work. Reagan was shot today. I realize that I must leave here and never come back. This morning, I see a hummingbird, and after it hummed in the azalea blossom, it perched on the end of a twig. I'd never seen a hummingbird in stillness. The stillness of the hummingbird allowed me to see into the eyes of the bird. This is when I felt humbled by the beautiful power of its being.

At the end of the spring semester, two pivotal things happened. First, my doctor prescribed a drug called Flagyl for a vaginal infection I had. After one pill, I knew the drug was toxic, stopped taking it and healed myself with garlic and goldenseal within three days. I had no doubt the drug was toxic. I had no doubt the herbs would heal. The feeling of having no doubt was new. I liked it. I didn't know where this feeling came from. I didn't inquire. I didn't even contemplate it that much. I now realize, of course, that this certainty was the healer within me, the not-yet-acknowledged connection to Source energy whose seeds of wisdom began to sprout that week. Tasting the herbs, absorbing their message into my cells awakened me to my healing nature. There was no one around to validate this experience. I didn't need validation. That's the nature of being certain, of feeling the truth. Wasn't it Gandhi who said, "Even if you are a minority of one, the truth is the truth."

The second thing that happened was an accident at one of the nuclear reactors at the Savannah River Plant. Radioactive tritium leaked into the atmosphere. The papers said it was "nothing harmful". I had read enough about nuclear contamination to know that there were no safe levels of radiation. I'd studied the subject since moving to the South. I'd followed waste trucks many mornings on my way to work; I had demonstrated at the Barnwell Nuclear Waste Site.

Did the accident cause me to leave the South? No. I had already made the choice. I knew that I had to leave. Just as I knew I had to stop taking the drug the doctor prescribed. Was the South itself toxic for me? No. It was my Petri dish; it was where I began to feel a place within myself that I could count on, where I made choices that were in my highest good. The contrast I experienced there helped me to understand what I did not want, which in turn guided me toward what I did want.

Was this conscious for me then? Not like it is now. But it was conscious enough that I made those choices. I moved north to study writing. I began to trust my intuition. I left Ken.

June '81

Perhaps I needed to leave a long time ago. I suppose I wanted some reassurance from Ken, to know that he understood why, not wanting to hurt him. But now I see how foolish this is. I've been living for his love. Foolish. I've been afraid that I would feel empty if I left him. Foolish. I've been waiting for the right moment. Foolish. It's raining now. He and I are at Standing Indian Campground outside Asheville where we rented a cabin. This will be our last time together before I drive north. He asked me last night why I needed a feminist environment to support my writing. "I just do," I said.

He's sitting on the porch of our cabin now. I walk down to the river, find a four-leaf clover. The river flows fast because of all the rain. I stare at one rock just beneath the swirl of white water. For a brief moment I see the beauty of everything.

Belief

When beliefs are not conscious, they still do their part in creating our life. It's a Wizard of Oz phenomenon. We think things just happen, such as the same relationship dynamic over and over (even though we choose new people), or the same job situation, or the same financial flow. "Why me?" is the common response, as if life is occurring without our consent, as if we are not creating it.

But when you pull back the curtain, you find that *you believe that you are worthy of exactly what you are getting.* It is true that only what we think is possible will occur in our life. Not only that, if we think something is possible without also feeling that it is, we will not manifest the thing we are so wanting.

Hence the necessity of examining our beliefs.

Joy cannot rise up when beliefs that joy is difficult to attain exist. Perhaps for moments, but not consistently. I've always wanted consistent joy. I know that's my true nature. So when my moment is less than joyous, I inquire. I ask. I work to shift from fear to love. The shift can happen in a moment, or it may take hours.

The Sparrows When It's -30

2009

It's winter solstice. I am blessed by the sparrows chirping as they hover in the dormant vines of the trumpet honeysuckle. They also nestle in the thicker branches of the bare forsythia hedge. Their chirping sounds like the little chicks crowded together at Easter for the children to see. It's constant. They swarm when startled. When they swarm, so do my ideas. When ideas are swarming, there's no articulation available, only a feeling of rich diversity, like an unharmed estuary.

Moments ago, one little sparrow just outside my office window closed his eyes briefly as the sun shone upon him. It's thirty below wind chill today in Iowa City and throughout the upper Midwest. Two starlings have joined the sparrows. The long-beaked starlings begin to eat the snow. I realize they must be thirsty, so I fill a large skillet with warm water and place it on the shoveled landing in the drive, where I scatter seed every few hours. A robin finds the water in less than two minutes. Then the starlings come, sit side by side on the edge of the skillet sipping the water.

I watch the birds all morning.

They connect me with my Being. I am a bird also. I feel the birds in my belly. I have always had this connection. It has grounded me in my journey through life. It may seem as though the birds are not much of a security net, but for me, they feel like an exquisite blanket woven out of soft, golden threads of light. They help me know who I am. They help me make choices. Because of their perfection, their sweetness, their power, I am able to feel my Being, which is where my Guidance lives. I'm able to feel my own perfection, sweetness and power. Thus, the birds absolutely assist the direction of my life.

Today, their exuberance (in spite of the cold) inspired me to begin again, to tap into the flow of this book, to trust my ability to allow words to take shape without me blocking them with thoughts I carry around from the past, which inevitably arise but which I now have power over. This is the power of choice, choosing my thoughts.

10.

Moving North to Study Writing

1982

My choice to go north to study writing after living in the South felt like freedom. It was the first time that my choice to change direction came from inside me, rather than from external expectations by others or society. I felt this in my body as I drove up Interstate 81, through Hazelton, Scranton, then into New York State. 81 North had an entirely different feeling than 81 South. More oxygen. The large hemlocks and hills emitted a feeling of strength. In the South, I felt weak.

Susan Griffin, author of *Women and Nature*, would be part of the visiting faculty at the Women's Writer's Center that fall. She was the reason I applied. How she used language made sense to me. Her account of how the Divine Feminine was ripped away from the consciousness of the dominant culture by folks such as Descartes stung with truth. On days when I forgot my deeper Self while living in the South, I grabbed her book.

Behind naming, beneath words, is something else.
An existence named unnamed and unnamable. We
give the grass a name, and earth a name. We
say grass and earth are separate. We know this
because we can pull the grass free of the earth
and see its separate roots — but when the grass is
free, it dies. We say the inarticulate have no
souls. We say the cow's eye has no existence
outside ourselves, that the red wing of the
blackbird has no thought, the roe of the salmon no
feeling, because we cannot name these.

I had to find my own voice. Studying with her would
help, I reasoned.

To test my resolve, the day I arrived in Cazenovia,
NY, I received a call from Western Carolina University
offering me a teaching fellowship for the academic year.
I had applied for that because Ken took a job there and
part of my pattern of decision-making was to keep as many
options open as possible. I don't remember exactly how
long I took to choose again, but I know it was only a matter
of hours when I called to turn it down.

Virginia Woolf & Me

The unanticipated ally awaiting me in upstate New York at The Women's Writer's Center was Virginia Woolf. I hadn't read her work until that winter in '82. When I read the first page of *To The Lighthouse*, a recognition took place. Yes, the long sentence astounded me. But it wasn't her sentence; it was her. I could feel her. I could imagine having written that sentence. During the time I read Virginia, I dreamed of my mother. She told me all she ever wanted was a room of her own, that the new brick ranch on the hill that she and Dad built wasn't large enough. (I hadn't yet read *A Room of One's Own.*)

The book of Virginia's I held most dear was *A Writer's Diary*, a compilation of her journals about her writing process that her husband, Leonard, edited after her death.

> Nov. 28th, 1928 Father's birthday. He would have been
> 96, yes, today; but mercifully was not. His life
> would have entirely ended mine. What would have
> happened? No writing, no books; inconceivable.

Again, her words sent a rush of recognition through my body; how brave of her to write this, how truthful.

* * *

Now, it's 2008. I'm reading *A Sketch of the Past*, her attempt to piece together the effect her childhood, including the rapes by her stepbrother, had upon her life. "Here I come to one of the memoir's difficulties," writes Woolf. "One of the reasons why, though I read so many, so many are failures. They leave out the person to whom things happened. The reason is that it is so difficult to describe any human being. So they say: 'This is what happened'; but they do not say what the person was like to whom it happened. And the events mean very little unless we know first to whom they happened. Who was I then?"

Virginia would take her life before she finished her memoir.

* * *

I am more than two decades beyond my year at the Women's Writer's Center. I am not who I was then. Yet, I am who I was then. My Being is not changed, though I am more fully embodied, more fully expressed. The explosion of language I seek right now, as hundreds of crows fly and land, fly and land outside my house on this cold January afternoon in Iowa, is the same explosion I first experienced at the writing center when suddenly the lyricism of my soul became visible on the page. Now, the explosion teases me, seems beyond my reach. I want the crows to help.

I am in two places at once. I am sitting here, with the crows, having fed Horton dinner, and I am in 1982, when, finally, though still precariously, I aligned with the desire to write that motivated me to go north and it was there that my words landed on the page with a power I had never imagined.

Christmas Eve

2009

The crows have come to feed this Christmas Eve. They are cautious at first. Many of them sit high up in the pin oaks, while one drops to the lowest limb to observe the seed scattered on the snow. The snow is fresh and light. It fell during the night. I shoveled a place for the seed first thing. The crows caw. The sun glistens on their black feathers making them blue.

Horton and I walk to Upper City Park. I plead to God (I feel like Virginia) to tell me why I am writing this book. What is its wisdom, its purpose?

This kind of self-reflection makes me nervous when I view the book through the eyes of literary critics. Oh, what a challenge to stay inside my Self and only view life through my own truth.

My Inner Being knows what art is and what it isn't. She knows what inspires and what doesn't, what's whole and what's incomplete.

Home from our walk.

Horton is snoring.

What perfection!

11.

Winning the Grant

1983

When the Women's Writer's Center moved from upstate New York to Provincetown, Massachusetts, I stayed behind because I had started teaching at Syracuse University. I realized soon after they moved that the support of the writer's community was essential to my newly formed voice, my newly formed narrative.

It was March of 1983. I had applied for an individual artist grant in poetry with New York State, but had not yet heard the results. If I won, I could live on that money. But I couldn't wait to find out. I had to quit my job. The urgency I felt to do this frightened me. I wasn't used to acting without approval. Desperate actions.

I had been teaching *Native Son*. Though my deeds weren't murderous like those of Bigger Thomas, still I felt like him: I understood the place deep inside where fear and alienation can overtake the heart. Where all sense of Self is eclipsed by a world where connection to Spirit doesn't exist. The isolation I felt in the classroom among the students who laughed at my empathy for Bigger, who said the book had no relevance to their future careers as doctors and dentists, propelled me to act.

I lied. I told the department chair I had a family emergency that would keep me in West Virginia for the rest of the semester. I left a message on his machine. I couldn't face him in person, the possible consequence on my career. I pretended I didn't care.

The lie I told my boss seemed absolutely necessary. I feared that if I didn't move to Provincetown with the women in whose company I found my new voice, I would lose what I had gained the year at the writer's center. The truth and perceptions, which surfaced as I wrote, would vanish. There was an authority in the words I had discovered — their pattern, image, and cadence led me back to some place real inside myself. A location that could possibly be my Soul, where the blueprint of who I was, was perfectly clear. I needed to touch that blueprint, to smell its ink, to trace its lines with my fingers. When I read the poems I submitted for the grant aloud to myself, whether in my office, my bedroom, or reciting in the car, for the first time in my life my voice filled the space. The words also filled my body; there were no empty corners for shame to grab hold and silence me. But this voice was new and fragile like a newborn baby. If I lost hold, I didn't want to live. Staying at my job, therefore, felt like death.

The day after I left the message for my boss, I drove from upstate New York to West Virginia down Interstate 81 through Pennsylvania, then west on I-40 from

Hagerstown into the blue Allegheny Mountains. Once I got to Cumberland, Maryland, I was almost home, only another thirty minutes on 220 South, a two-lane road where the houses become progressively smaller and more decrepit. I began to recite my poem called "Civilization":

> The land is far away from here
> There is space there
> Still wild
> And it is inside me
> So I want it on the outside
> But it is not here.

> Here, there is North American Van Lines blue
> More of a background than opera music
> Except for American flags
> And the woman in the trench coat
> Left a trail of pink perfume
> Down the sidewalk
> As the jacked-up car blared its radio.

> Quiet calls forth something different in everyone
> And yet the same
> For it can't be explained.
> And then, if you want to stare out the window for a year
> What you remember will be of use
> And in exchange for your impulse to share
> A good supply of wood.

The moon is waning this day in July
After Skylab falls to Earth.
Hospitals and facts
Freedom to just be
Away from advertised domesticity.
Glittering above the hayfield
A midsummer fog.

The mountain air flooded my senses after crossing into West Virginia. The air was magnificent. It smelled like the place beneath moss in the woods when you lift it off a rock and put your nose to the roots. A rich, earthy smell tinged with sweetness.

Dad opened the front door and waved just as I drove past the school and started up the hill to our house. He must have been watching for me. I pulled into the carport. I noticed how my breath became small then, like a little bird, as soon as I turned off the motor. Here I am, I thought. But it was more than a thought. Being here felt like being stopped, as if I had reached down inside myself and picked up a heavy steel anchor and thrown it overboard. I was attached to this place — the land, the house — attached in the sense that I knew it more completely than anything in the world. Being anchored here, especially to the land, had always made me feel like I belonged somewhere on the planet. My attachment was also to Dad, his money, his concern, all the things that seemed like love. But I hadn't visited since my year of writing and something had changed. Although my new writing had not yet pierced the wall of forgetting surrounding the life I had lived in this house, my imagination had soared into new territory, and I had begun to feel as if I could be anchored to myself instead of to this place, instead of to Dad. My poems felt alive, as if they had filtered through my experiences from heaven. Language was coming back to me from somewhere. Or I was coming back to myself through language. Sitting in the silent car, I felt distinct from this place and from Dad for the first time. I had something of my own now. I wondered whether or not I should share my writing with Dad, or keep it to myself.

I heard Dad's slippers scuffing the cement sidewalk from the front door to the carport but I couldn't see him yet. "Keep it to yourself," I heard inside my head.

I looked up at him walking towards me as he had done it seemed a hundred times before in exactly the same way, his body appearing slumped, tired, needing my love. He wore a long-sleeved white shirt, cuffs rolled up to his elbows, and old jeans. His hands were covered with old age spots but looked strong. At seventy-two, he still had no gray hair.

"Welcome home," he said, as he stepped up to the car.

"Hey Dad," I said. We hugged. In this moment I felt as if our molecules mixed, some part of his cells reached out and grabbed the edges of mine. We were invisibly merged again. "It's so much warmer here," I said, breaking away from his body. The thoughts I had so clearly formed while sitting in the car were melting now, coming apart, losing their cohesiveness. I could find a word here and there, but their logic, or rather their truth, had gone away. It's only temporary, I thought. I just need to adjust, get some water, unpack.

"You hungry?" Dad asked. "I have a steak for you if you want it."

"I need some water," I said. "Some of our spring water."
I picked up my duffel bag and put it over my shoulder.

"There's plenty of water. Let me get your bag."

"It's okay. I got it."

"How long did it take you?"

"Nine hours. It always takes nine hours, Dad."

"Look here," he said, pointing to the yard beside the
carport. "Your daffodils are blooming."

Eloise, my stepmother, sat in her recliner in the
living room with the heavy red-flowered draperies pulled,
watching television. Her emphysema had worsened right
after Dad sold the store. I figured this happened partly
because Dad's presence had a smothering affect on her. She
was much less active than she had been. She looked up and
smiled at me. I walked over, bent down and hugged her,
stood beside her and watched *M.A.S.H.* for a few minutes.

"I had your room cleaned," she said.

"Thanks," I said.

The next day, around noon, when Eloise was at the
beauty shop and Dad was delivering Lion's Club mints to local
businesses, I called the grant office in New York to find out if
I'd won. The mailing had probably gone out the day before to
my New York address. I was to meet Dad at the bank in town
at one o'clock to transfer money into my account.

The only phone in the house was a black rotary
phone which sat on the old buffet in Eloise's sewing room.
When I was nine and Christine was my stepmother, the
sewing room had been my bedroom. It was pink then.
Now, the walls were yellow with built-in bookshelves

where windows had been. They were covered over by the addition Dad built when he married Eloise. In this airless room, I dialed the 212 number in Manhattan. A woman answered. I told her that I was traveling and wouldn't get my mail for weeks. She said, "Just a minute and I'll find out if you're one of the winners."

I waited. I stared at the thread Eloise had arranged by color on the shelf next to her machine. The tiny spools were stacked on a five-tier metal rack made specifically for thread. There must have been a hundred spools, all colors. She tried to teach me to sew. I had pretended that I wanted to learn in order to please her, when actually I hated it. I hated everything about it. The stuffy room, cutting out patterns, threading the bobbins. And most of all I hated the way homemade clothes looked. I turned off the light and bathed in the absolute darkness. I liked that better. The buffet I leaned against had belonged to my real mother. She used it to separate the kitchen from the dining area in our first house beside the store. With my fingernail I scraped what seemed like old kitchen grease from its wooden corner.

The woman was back. I heard her pick up the receiver; I felt her breath. "I'm happy to tell you that you're one of the lucky ones," she said. "Usually, I have to disappoint people." When I heard "happy" I wanted that woman to squeeze through the phone line and be with me. She was so kind, and loving. I had won. I didn't know how to feel. She could help me understand that nothing bad would happen to me because I'd won. But most of these thoughts I am describing, these desires for normalcy, were unconscious. I could not feel success. Just like one can't feel a pin prick to a paralyzed limb. I didn't realize then the degree to which I went numb. All I knew was that winning had somehow swept away the anchor to my Self that I had begun to feel by writing the poems that won.

"Are you sure?" I asked.

"Yes, Nancy Swisher. You're on the list. Congratulations!"

"Thank you," I said. I didn't want to hang up. I wanted to ask her to stay on the line, to let me tell her that hearing I'd won suddenly terrified me. I wanted to tell her I didn't know why, to ask her if she could help me understand this unexpected numbness, this ice-cold fear, which flooded over and through me. Had any of the other winners responded like me?

I flipped on the light, hung up the phone. "I won!" I shouted. I jumped up and down. In spite of the terror, I tried to act happy. Perhaps the fear I felt wasn't real; it made no sense. My poems had been chosen. My voice had been heard. I looked out the kitchen window at our mountain. "I won!" I said. I stared long enough to become part of the mountain, the sun, the air, to absorb their calm. The trees were bare, but swollen with spring buds where new leaves formed, the tips of their branches reddening, the color of Merlot. At the base of the mountain our white Methodist church in the valley looked bright in the spring sun, its stained-glass windows shining magenta, green, turquoise and gold. I wondered if the painting of Jesus with the lambs was still in there. I hadn't been inside the church for years.

Dad stood in the shade of a large pine tree outside the Farmers and Merchants Bank on Main Street. I parked across the street from him. He waved, motioned me over.

I was bound to him once again. The Self which my poems had begun to illuminate was hiding. The success frightened her. Childlike, I ran across the street to tell him. "Dad," I said, "I won the New York grant!" I was thirty-two and felt eleven.

"The what?" he said.

"The grant for my writing. I won. They only pick twenty people from the whole state of New York," I said. He had turned to go into the bank. I trailed behind him.

"That's great, honey," he said. "I'll put a write-up in the paper later today. The publisher's a friend of mine. How much money do you need?"

I heard the voice of the woman in New York. I heard her say, "You're one of the lucky ones." I imagined her beautiful smiling face. I wanted to hold onto her words. I could do that by never forgetting them. Now, I needed to think about money. How much did I need? How does one determine that? I shouldn't have needed any money from my father at this age, yet I felt powerless over his endless offering.

Blue Heron

2009

I saw the heron just in time because I felt disconnected from my Soul, flipped into a sort of dead zone, you could say, where the vibrancy and even ecstasy of life seems to be behind a closed door.

No, not depression, but a conscious choice to transform an old pattern of focusing on loss, and all my skills couldn't get it to fall away, not this day, not this morning, though Horton remained the perfect Being that he is.

I walked around the dog park, head down, nothing to look at, the eagles have gone north for spring, no leaves yet, a killdeer on warmer mornings has beckoned me twice, sounding Dad's spirit, memory of him teaching me about the bird's hatching behaviors.

But on this day, silently, up from the river bank the blue heron rose, head pulled back, legs outstretched, alone it flew towards me as I looked up and prayed for my heart to open, for my body to feel the heron's body, for my Spirit to merge with its Spirit. Let us touch, I silently pleaded, as if to a lover. The bird flew slowly, circling overhead, hearing my call and giving me the Presence I needed to pop through the illusion of my closed heart. I was connected to me again.

12.

Wellfleet Therapist

What led me to seek a therapist for the first time in my life was a letter I received from my father. I'd been living on Cape Cod for a year. The natural beauty supported my Spirit, but I felt rather helpless when it came to standing behind my winning poems. I didn't send them out for publication. I did a couple readings, but that was it. I knew that had my writer friends just won the New York writing grant I did (it was quite prestigious), they would have put all of their effort into publishing a book of poems as quickly as possible. The fact that I didn't even consider doing this seemed normal to me. I felt my inertia but couldn't name it. I felt like hiding. Why? I began to wonder.

My housemate Kim and I sat in the sun in the backyard admiring our small garden of tomatoes, eggplant, marigolds and basil. It was 1984 — the summer Jesse Jackson ran for president. Kim and I rented a television to watch his speech.

Dad's letter began with a description of his garden — the abundant Silver Queen sweet corn, the perfect Kentucky Wonder pole beans. He had taken a fishing trip

119

through the Trough, a section of the Potomac River he taught me to canoe. The Lion's Club picnic was a huge success. He provided the chicken. Towards the end of this letter, he offered a piece of his philosophy, something he also did frequently — "Just be thankful life is no worse," he said.

After reading these words, the sun seemed to disappear along with any sense of happiness I had been feeling. For the first time in my life I began to consider how deeply influenced I had been by him.

* * *

The therapist had short, thick white hair and wore silver jewelry. Her summer house sat on the dunes above the Atlantic. I could see the dark blue ocean beyond her living room window as we walked into her office. I tried to keep a vision of the ocean inside myself as I sat across from her.

"Tell me a little history," she said. I had my story. Mother died when I was seven is how my story always began. I talked about the beauty of Dad's land and the nurturance I received from Nature. How Dad did the best he could, considering Mom died and left him with two daughters. I told her about the store and how much I loved it. I told her I was a writer, that since winning the grant I couldn't write and felt a deep sense of shame, which I didn't understand.

"Go on," she said. She had a look on her face that made me nervous but I decided this subtle grin reflected her knowledge and caring, rather than her own protection from what my truth might be.

"I feel like there's something inside me that I'm not aware of. I never feel like I'm totally who I really am," I said. The expression on her face didn't change as I spoke. Could I say the word? Was she really going to understand and help? "Sometimes I wonder if my dad touched me in an inappropriate way that I don't remember," I said.

My eyes burned. My vision blurred. Her white hair blended into the beige wall. I sunk into myself.

She straightened her husky, expert body in the brocade wing chair. Would she respond? Or simply stare me down. Time seemed to stop between my words and hers. I had never spoken these words to anyone including myself until this moment. My fragile sense of truth I handed to her.

"You're much too creative for that to have happened," she said.

When I try to remember what happened next in the session, I go blank. I felt shocked, I think. But the shock was strangely mixed with relief about not being as damaged as I thought. I probably smiled at her. I know I scheduled an appointment for the following week. I think she told me I had self-esteem issues and that we could work on those.

I drove back to my cottage. I rolled down all my windows, breathed in the smell of the scrub pines nestled tightly in the sand along Route 6 between Wellfleet and North Truro.

Part of me felt relieved. Another part, buried in the cells of my body — my belly, my vagina, my neck, my breasts, my nipples, my stomach and liver — was devastated, as if a bomb had been detonated by the therapist's words. The damage of this explosion was psychic and emotional. It couldn't be seen or heard by anyone, including me.

I allowed the Wellfleet therapist to determine my truth that day. I had learned long ago to permit my own reality to be overridden. After this therapy session, my full awareness of my childhood remained dormant for another six years.

Although I tried to bring the voice of my younger self into the light when I wrote in my journal, I couldn't hold onto her truth all by myself. I needed an enlightened witness. I needed another person capable of exploring that dark, unconscious place with me. This particular expert, who taught other therapists and was widely published, couldn't do that. I wanted to say during that first session, "I'm not trying to be a victim; I'm just trying to understand why I don't send out my poems. It makes no sense. It's as if when I try to think about the act of publishing them, having them be seen, I immediately do something that has nothing to do with my poems. There's a click in my brain, a switch, something flips it and any idea of a manuscript disappears."

I could not say these words. I wasn't yet conscious enough. They were there though. They were. The drive for truth was always there.

The Paradox of Memory

Because I could not remember what had happened to me when Dad and I wrote my sixth-grade essay, I experienced parts of life behind a veil, much like Virginia Woolf describes her cotton wool experience in *A Sketch of the Past*, the memoir that she never finished because she killed herself.

She, too, felt cut off from her full Presence; powerless, afraid to make the connections, of becoming incapacitated by the feelings associated with her traumatic past. She felt encased in cotton wool, separate, not connected.

She used the term 'non-being' to describe this state. I like this phrase. For me, non-being is when you go through the motions of life, talk about a subject you have absolutely no interest in, surf the Internet rather than be present, eat to push down the unwanted feelings. In contemporary psychology it's called dissociation. Spiritually, it is a state of perceived disconnection from Source that creates aloneness, emptiness, and a desperate need to get rid of these feelings. A typical way to do this is by staying very busy.

The space of non-being also creates a need to find answers outside yourself because you are cut off from your innate wisdom, your own spiritual knowledge, and your soul's voice. You sense this, begin to seek guidance to redirect your life to the place within that you long to feel: a place of wholeness, joy and peace.

Unfortunately, some professional guidance leads you to believe that another person has the answers for you. Like Freud did for Virginia. Just when she began to make sense of the connection between her childhood abuse, her depression, and the voices in her head, she capitulated to Freud, the expert. He had decided that reports of incest were fantasies of wish fulfillment. Virginia wondered at the end of her life whose view was correct: hers or his? She struggled to establish her own knowing but eventually wavered and accepted Freud's. This meant that she would have to see herself as mad, just as her stepbrothers who molested her had said she was.

When the Wellfleet therapist had no room in her psyche for my intuitive hunch, because I was hanging on to it by a thread, and because she was the expert, I let go of my own wisdom for a time, remained disconnected from those young parts of myself, which, in turn, formed a wall between me and me.

What Has Been

2009

I recently had lunch with a friend who said that her guru taught her that the past is a lesser form of consciousness. I would agree. However, I would not agree that by meditating hours per day the past can be erased and healed, that the subconscious patterns of belief will therefore not surface during life when the perfect situation arises to trigger them into action. The younger parts of our self who still hold tightly to past beliefs, thoughts and feelings, must be integrated in order to transcend to higher states of consciousness. Otherwise, what is called premature transcendence or spiritual bypassing occurs.

Thinking about what has been, turning to look backward into the past can indeed be an obstacle to connecting with Spirit and to the full Presence of our evolutionary Self, so I make a 'note to self' that when I look into the past it is for the purpose of illuminating the human journey of my Spirit, to see how subconscious patterns played out, to let go of false beliefs, to lean more fully into the Holy Self that I am, to feel my divinity, and to love all the parts who may still feel unseen and unloved.

I go to the dog park to ask the eagles for guidance. Today, they say, "Have fun!" I realize from the Eagle Wisdom that the voices that had been swirling in my head are ego (programmed) voices — *You must write this way, It is not literature, It is not self-help.* (I think of Virginia's voices and how she struggled with them.)

My transformation right now is to become so present to the Presence that I clearly see that the programmed voices are simply not mine, but thoughts I made up due to early circumstances and experiences.

The eagles always provide the power of Spirit necessary for me to realize what's true.

How would Virginia capture the messiness of how a person moves from confusion to clarity? By creating a character, of course. At the end of her life, though, she tried to make sense of her voices through memoir rather than fiction. She knew intuitively that they came from her early abuse experiences; however, she was unable to stand by her truth in the face of Freud's fantasy theories and Hitler's possible invasion of England. She didn't have anyone who could embrace her truth with her. Eventually, we all must have wise and loving support for our lives. We can't be fully ourselves without each other. And by wise and loving, I mean someone who understands that we are spiritual beings having a human experience. Someone who understands the shadow. Someone who knows that we must walk though our darkness, feel it, release it, and receive its power into our psyche in order to be whole.

13.

The Ashram

1985

My last night on Cape Cod, I dreamed my father was kissing my neck. I know this because I found the journal entry years later. At the time, I dismissed any significance.

Hurricane Gloria had moved up the East Coast to Cape Cod, putting Provincetown under warning. The hurricane's strength fizzled before arriving, though it did bring wind and rain. Kim and I had gone out to buy a pint of Häagen Dazs Swiss Vanilla Almond to celebrate my last night. Many people were in the street, playing in the storm. It was October, so most of the summer residents had left. The town began to feel like home again to the writers and artists who resided year round, sensing at last the emptiness of the winter season that fueled their creative spirits.

The next morning, I drove to the Berkshires, a four-hour drive west on I-90. I was moving into Kripalu Yoga Ashram for the three-month Spiritual Lifestyle Training program.

* * *

My friend Debbie, who traveled Europe with me ten years prior, surprised me when she quit her college teaching job in psychology in order to move into Kripalu. Her move into the ashram seemed out of character. She was my most goal-oriented friend. When she set her mind to do something, to hike a trail in the Alps, for instance, she wouldn't stop until she reached her destination, no matter what. I found this aspect of her personality challenging. Irritating, to be honest. At the same time I admired it.

I, on the other hand, would prefer sitting among the alpine wildflowers, absorbing color, resting, breathing Swiss air. Then walking some more, if I felt like it. I didn't think of myself as goal-oriented. I had my writing, which was a way of life more than a goal.

My goals, had I been able to give them words, were consciousness, balance, and truth more than the writing on the page. I still believed that matter and spirit opposed one another. If I had a goal, I couldn't be in the moment, like in the Alps. Debbie pushed forward to the top; I wanted to sit, stare at the purple. To me, the purple was the moment, the point of connection to something bigger. Goals ripped that something from me; I always opted for being in the moment. I didn't know how to create unity between the inner form of Spirit and the outer world of form. That's what I told myself, anyway.

* * *

Debbie had cornered me when I visited her that August to get away from the crowds in Provincetown. We took a walk down Hawthorne Road, where Nathaniel Hawthorne's little red house stands in the field above Lake Mahkeenac.

We stopped to look at Hawthorne's house, briefly sharing about the year we both read *The Blithedale Romance*.

Debbie turned to me. "Nancy," her voice deepened as she stared me in the eye with such intensity I needed to take a step back, "living here will support and nurture the place inside you where your writing comes from." Her eyes didn't move from mine as she waited for a response. I knew very well what she meant. What I couldn't imagine was living in an ashram. (The thought of it.) Was I imagining it negatively because I concerned myself with what others would think of me? What my friends in P-town would think? What my family would think? As Debbie continued to explain the spiritual teachings that formed the basis of the ashram, I barely heard her, for the worried voices in my head were too loud to ignore. I did, however, allow her truth to influence me.

* * *

I moved into the brick building (a former Jesuit monastery built in the '60s) on the hill asking two questions: Who am I? Why am I here? Though I always maintained an experience of Being, whether or not I could stand there solidly within myself was unpredictable. In other words, I didn't have the skills, tools, a mentor, or an enlightened witness to show me how to go inward in a way that I could count on, or how to align my human self with my spiritual Self. I needed a practice.

* * *

My room, which I shared with another woman, had no windows to the outside, though it had a window to a larger dormitory space on the floor below me. It also had air ducts that pumped fresh air from the outside. We each had a single futon on the floor, one nightstand between our beds, two closets, and a hall bath that we shared with many other women. I had lived alone since leaving college (except for the brief time with Ken). I believed that I needed to live alone in order to feel who I was, in order to write, in order to create peace of mind.

I now had to reconcile these beliefs about my life and myself with my new choice to live in an ashram. It was a choice. No one forced me. I could have applied to an MFA program. I could have taught college English again. There were options.

Debbie's certainty affected me though. There are times we need others' certainty when our own is not yet solid. Hers was the nudge that helped me choose.

* * *

After living at the ashram for a few months, I attended a workshop for residents about manifesting one's vision. This appealed to me since I didn't have a vision for my life beyond the day I was in and maybe the next. I thought I should and that I must learn how. The woman teaching was very dynamic and loving. When she spoke about the structural tension necessary to create your vision, I interrupted her, asked her to repeat that. She said, "There is a structural tension between where you are now, and what you want to create. It's important to feel that tension in order to draw your vision to you." I didn't know whether I totally understood what she meant, but I comprehended enough to make sense for myself. I knew that living in an ashram was not where I ultimately belonged.

Total devotion to the guru seemed foolish to me. I did what I had to do to fit in, actually enjoyed the yoga, communal meals, and some of the guru's teachings, but spent much of my free time in my room devoting myself to my own thoughts about what felt true, and to my writing. I knew that something kept me from my vision, stood in the way, invisible and unnamed. I desired more than anything for what blocked my forward movement in life to suddenly surface. Like mushrooms after rain.

The Ashram Journals

I must learn to let my Light come through me as the guru does. Is this why I am here? To unveil that Light? To learn how to do that?

Every morning the crows caw. I would be satisfied to be a crow.

I sit under the blue spruce. Smell the dirt. Birds so small they fool me into thinking they are dried leaves. Wind in big tree. Blue mountains. I imagine writing as spiritual activity.

I am writing. I am writing to protect my soul from having no space.

Om Namo Bhagavate Vasudevaya (this is the mantra we chant).

My jaw needs stretching.

I saw a shooting star with a tail in the morning sky between Orion and Venus.

In Satsanga (a Sanskrit word meaning 'in the company of the highest truth'), Gitanand spoke of the theory of dissipative structures and how transformation happens within us. Much of his teaching comes from *The Aquarian Conspiracy,* but what is amazing to me is that here such transformative energy abounds. I did not know this when I came. I came here to change. But I was thinking of change on such a superficial level, which then I did not realize. I want to be centered in my Light, in the light of Love. But right now I feel weak, frightened, and ignorant about my life and life in general. Old feelings and old ways of thinking come through my mind and I know they are no longer real and true but at the same time my new strengths aren't yet here.

I get a massage from Varuni. She works on my lower back. Then puts heat on my sacrum and leaves the room. My head face down in the headrest. I feel as if I've been transported to heaven, sustained on pure Love energy and nothing else.

Two hours later, I have compacted the garbage in the dark, wearing my favorite yellow pants; finished the cauliflower order by cutting fourteen gallons for tomorrow's lunch. The dining chapel is quiet, except for a random whisper. Part of being here is witnessing the winter thaw. The hillsides are green and it's only January 20th.

I am learning not to need what I do not have and that this is not resignation but fulfillment. Still not totally clear. Still not a way of being.

I know the truth that by changing yourself you can change the world. Sometimes being here makes me feel so cut off from the world and usually it is a joyous and understandable experience, intentionally undergone by

134 | Nancy Swisher

me to transform myself. But other times, like the last couple of days, I have felt on the edge of insanity here, as if everything goes in circles, not spirals, that no one here shares my perspective, or passion, or love of the world. And I do — I love the beauty of the world, and the passion and the truths that people try for. Why am I in this ashram? Where do I connect with the world from here? The connections feel broken. And once again, I realize this feeling is not new. It is an old feeling from childhood or before.

I like it when, in the early morning, the snow looks blue.

The strong feeling comes again. Why am I here? Will I some day have the space to look back on this time and read, "On Dec. 28th the feeling repeated itself and I tried to watch it. Not to panic. Not to run. To see all my actions. Not to reject my confused self. The rice fast makes everything faster and faster till there's no use trying to see right from wrong. I surrender to my life. That is what I surrender to." Art is not living. It is the use of living.

This morning the tired past came up. I remember telling my first homeopath how I was tired a lot. Not knowing then that it is connected to not expressing or claiming my Essence, my power. This morning the connection arose clearly. Why do I feel this way? When one is committed to a spiritual path everything changes. Fear becomes a steppingstone for change. Breath becomes life.

Gurudev spoke of newness and how when we are fully present every moment is new. When he speaks I am taken to a place of truth. In my astrology reading with Mary, she said that I am searching for my own mastership, that I am beyond having a guru in the sense that I am on my way to my own mastery. She said it's not wrong for me to get initiated but not necessary.

I have now eaten miso soup for breakfast and put tahini sauce, sesame seeds, and raisins on my rice. For lunch I ate greens with dressing, rice and cauliflower sauce. Then a cookie. I break the fast too abruptly, maybe, but I feel my system starting to want a variety of foods. The collards are most satisfying.

The Paris Review returned my writing, but said to send them more. I became disturbed by this and ate an apricot bar, which I had covered with Saran Wrap to save and possibly not eat at all.

I awaken with a sore throat and it doesn't take me long to realize it's fear. What I'm learning here is to be effective with my energy, to focus it, to move through the material world rather than get lost in it.

Sickness comes to the body and immune system because we do not challenge our perception of self as victim.

I need to walk. The snapdragons are blooming. Their vibrational essence heals the jaw.

The sky is busy with planes at 11:00 p.m. I stand on the porch of this large brick ashram, having not gone to hear the guru tonight. Instead, I seek to feel my Self inside my self, to breathe into my abdomen, which is free of doubt. I feel my own energy as mine, connected to Source, not to a guru. One shooting star. Crickets beneath the bush.

Equanimity

At the ashram, the guru spoke of equanimity. I learned the word there, as it applied to how I met the moment. I practiced bringing forth my full Presence, whether chopping tomatoes, meditating, or writing. During my last year, however, I began to feel the limitations of that environment. I was attracted in another direction, seeking, always seeking the expression of my Essence, the understanding of why it has felt so difficult to do so, to bring my Self into the world. When the programming of the conditioned mind is transformed, a continual flow of Love moves into the world through us as we see fit. A sentence, a kiss, a dog park visit, talking with the eagles, chewing each bite of food forty times, silence, hello to a stranger — all Love. None better than the other. Equanimity.

Ground of Being

2009

If the author of a book doesn't write the book, is it really a book? We should have a name for those books, the ones someone else writes for a person, other than 'book'. Books are meant to come from the ground of being of the writer, a transmission, from the place between writer and written, where the invisible meets the visible and one's consciousness occurs the moment the word comes onto the page.

What do I mean by ground of being? What I mean is a place inside yourself where you know who you are. I experienced my ground of being this morning at the dog park. I found a little yellow wild flower that I've been picking and looking at every spring of my life since I was a toddler. It's one of my favorites. When I found it this morning, and picked it and touched it and looked at it, my ground of being spoke the words I'm writing now. This is my ground of being.

When I passed the family of geese a few weeks ago, tears came to my eyes as I felt their family, the baby geese, the parents. I wept. That was my ground of being. My ground of being speaks from my Soul. Someone who doesn't write their own book is not sharing their ground of being. They may be sharing information, but there's a huge difference.

14.

The Albany Seminar

1990

I still lived at Kripalu when I learned about Landmark Education Seminars. A man named Daniel, who lived at the ashram though he shared openly that he didn't subscribe to the idea of a guru or the spiritual teachings of the yogic lifestyle, was actively involved with Landmark and encouraged some of the residents to attend the Albany seminar. Like all newly introduced fads, talk about Landmark quickly spread through the community. There was the time when macrobiotics was new and exciting and everyone tried it; there were new meditation techniques visiting swamis brought; Ayurvedic consultations; Dr. Sarno's back pain book; new hip-opening postures. The expansion of mind, body and spirit that I was exposed to in my four years was phenomenal. The difference between Landmark and these other trends was that Landmark came from outside, not from the guru or any senior resident. The other difference was that Landmark had a charismatic leader of its own; its own philosophy, its own language; its own code of behavior.

There were residents who believed doing anything outside the ashram was wrong. And there were those of us, a minority, who didn't have as narrow a focus. I met Daniel initially in the copy room. He introduced himself, then right away began to speak about the seminar, which a group of residents was going to that night in Albany. Although he seemed a bit preachy, the language he used interested me. Ideas like "living as your word" and "living as your commitment" resonated with me.

At the ashram, the words of the individual were not as valued as the words of the guru. Also, the words of the individual began to sound like the words of the guru. The focus was on being totally content with the moment. In contrast, the purpose of Landmark was to provide structures for the individual to connect to the larger external world of goals, accomplishment, success, relationship, and money.

When I attended my first seminar as a guest, I knew that I wanted to join. I wanted to feel certainty and empowerment, confidence and success. They promised to deliver. I believed them. Their words became a better match for me than the guru's words. It was as if I had used his words as much as I could. I had incorporated his words (the ones that rang true) into my being. I needed new ones. I didn't yet realize the words I longed for were within me.

I soon worked my way up the pecking order at Landmark.

I took all of their programs — the Forum, the 6-Day, Mastery of Empowerment, the Communication Course — and decided to train to become a leader in their organization. The hours I volunteered — driving to Boston, leading guest rooms, enrolling the quota to become an Introduction to the Forum Leader — convinced me this was my path.

The winter of 1990, I accepted a request from the seminar leader in Albany to manage her seminar. That particular seminar was called "Accomplishment". Managing meant I sat in the back of the room in a tall black director's chair overseeing the other volunteers and empowering Sarah, who stood in front of the crowd of approximately one hundred people: doctors, lawyers, journalists, mechanics, mothers, teachers, real estate agents — all kinds of people from all walks of life attended, the common thread being a desire for greater meaning and purpose in their lives.

I enjoyed being the manager. I was good at it. The next step up in the organization was seminar director. Sarah encouraged me to do that. I thought I might.

On this particular night, the seminar was half over. We had just finished the break when a young woman to my left towards the front of the room stood up to share. She began to speak about her one-year-old child, a girl, whom she had left with her estranged husband — the child's father — for an afternoon the day before. The woman began to share in an intense, urgent fashion. She said, "I think he's abusing my daughter. Her cry was different. There was something different in the sound of her cry."

One of Landmark's theories about human beings is that "We are not our stories." The leaders encourage people, many times rather forcefully, to let go of whatever their story about their past is. They distinguish seeing the self as psychological from seeing the self as ontological. The psychological assessment, in their view, invites the question "What's wrong with me?". Whereas an ontological assessment invites a person to live according to "being their word".

"That's just your story," Sarah said to the woman.

"But what if I'm right?" the young woman asked. "What if he is abusing my child?"

"You're making up a story that you are empowering," Sarah insisted.

They went back and forth like this until the woman surrendered to the leader's point of view and took a seat.

During this interchange, it was as if my consciousness escaped from the top of my head, floated above the participants and into the body and mind of this young woman desperately seeking her truth. For some unknown and inexplicable reason, I believed the woman. I could feel the truth of what she said. Something in her voice as she spoke about her baby caused me to experience a knowing inside that her child was being abused. I didn't understand at the time how this could be. I didn't understand why I bothered to give it so much attention. But, with the same certainty that I knew the chair I sat on was black, I knew her hunch was correct.

Witnessing the more powerful organizational words overtake the less powerful intuitive words felt familiar to me. A lost voice, a voice not yet empowered to trust its own source of truth, its own source.

My Silence

At this point in my life, a smile still replaced my truth. One of the patterns of my conditioning was connecting outwardly with a smile while being disconnected inwardly from myself. I'm sure I smiled as usual at the end of the seminar during the closing meeting with Sarah and the other volunteers. The knowing I felt when I heard the young woman's words about her child occurred intuitively. My conscious mind was not involved. I did not know how to stand behind my intuition. Not in a group like this. That I kept silent did not feel good to me though. My sleep was disturbed that night.

It was this young woman's story, however, that gave me the gift of this moment in time, when I felt not only my own intuition, but also a sense of spiritual connection and guidance more real than in previous similar moments in my life.

I began to listen — to listen within.

After days and weeks I clearly heard that my path in life was a path of healing and transformation, for others, and myself, and that this organization was not where I should be. So I quit.

Segue

At my last Satsanga with the guru, I raised my hand to share. He called on me. I walked to the front of the room to sit beside him. I began by thanking him for creating such an amazingly transformational place, the ashram, for me to grow. Although I was quite nervous, having never gone to the front of the Satsanga to ask a question in all the time I lived there, I noticed an odd blankness behind his eyes, as if he were not there. His response to me was, "What are you running away from?" I remained firm, saying, "I'm not running away from anything. I'm moving towards myself."

I had wanted someone else to tell me who I was — the guru, the empowered people at Landmark. But no one can do that. I moved closer to me from those experiences but it was I who made choice after choice to stay or leave, to listen to the Being I am or to others' self-proclaimed authority.

Tom

The writer in me says I can't bring Tom into the book because that would require describing him and our marriage and it would be too much for the purpose of this book. The healer and teacher in me disagree.

I moved in with Tom when I moved out of Kripalu in 1990. We fell in love. We had shared a carpool to and from Albany for the Landmark seminars. He also lived at Kripalu for the four years I lived there. I treated his colds with homeopathic remedies, as I did for all the residents, but we never talked much while at the ashram.

It was while having a late night breakfast at Howard Johnson's on the way home from one of those seminars that I saw the Light around Tom's head and began to feel my heart open to him.

Eventually, we married. We stayed married for thirteen years. Our souls intertwined.

Had I not created a safe home with him, had he not loved me so deeply and unconditionally, I'm not sure my healing would have unfolded as gently as it did.

Formless Form

2009

The rain was heavy last night but the tornadoes missed Iowa City. I take Horton to the section of the dog park for unsocial dogs, not because he's unsocial but because that section is less muddy. The grass is very green, wet, with white clovers blooming like a carpet; the air has a special feel. More oxygen, more clarity, more energy in the wake of the powerful Midwest storm.

Horton gravitates to the edge, where he nibbles the tall grass along the fence. I walk to the middle of the field, hold my arms outstretched to catch the full feeling of wind, moisture, and early summer heat.

Suddenly, I begin to cry. I miss my father (who died last year at the age of 98). "I miss you," I say, wiping my tears beneath my sunglasses.

Horton, still at the other end of the park, looks up. "Come here, Horton. I need you."

I laugh at myself, how dramatic I can be, a drama Horton adjusts to because he is so totally loyal.

As Horton runs to me, I realize my tears are not that I miss my father but that they are an acknowledgment of his presence with me right then. I take a few seconds to fully realize this. Shortly, I shift from "I miss you" to "Hi Dad."

His love is palpable.

Sunday is Father's Day. It makes sense he would be here now, not only for the occasion but to help me realize my true connection to All That Is.

You see, I have no doubt about his presence when he comes. He feels so real. You may say, *How do you know it's not just your imagination?*

Ah, but the imagination is the Universe flowing through me. Dad is part of the Universe now. He is formless form.

15.

Finding My Voice

1992

Betsy was not a traditional therapist like the one I saw in Wellfleet. She was a healer and spirituality-based counselor who specialized in the metaphysical nature of trauma. She had studied with many of the leading-edge therapists, such as David Calof and Christine Courtois; she had immersed herself in the work of Alice Miller and she had developed her own spiritual connection with many of the Ascended Masters. I was ready to take a chance with someone new to guide me on my healing journey.

I drove ninety minutes through the Berkshire Hills to get to her house, up and down and through the woods. I would usually see a bear, a fox, a turkey or some other beautiful animal or bird as I drove.

On that first meeting, Betsy opened the front door of her house before I even knocked. She wore long, beaded earrings in a Native American design and a purple tee shirt with a large snowy owl printed on the front. I knew right away I liked her.

We walked upstairs to her office. At one end of the room under a skylight, there was a five-foot-long table filled with crystals, feathers, and all sorts of sacred objects. We sat at the other end of the room.

I sat down on the couch across from her. From there I could see the beautiful table of crystals. She made me tea.

She pressed the record button on her recorder and we began my first session. I don't remember the first question Betsy asked but I do remember my answer. "When I think about where to begin my healing, I always see an image of my sixth-grade essay. I always feel like something happened at that time but I don't know what."

"Do you still have that essay?"

"Yes, I do."

"Bring it with you next week."

I had carried the essay with me in a box of keepsakes for thirty years, along with my mother's handkerchiefs, my grandfather's chalk pastels, my pink and white beaded newborn baby bracelet from the hospital nursery, a smooth rock from our land, and two baby books my mother made, filled with photos and locks of my hair held down with Scotch tape.

* * *

The following week I began by saying, "Something happened then." (I had no idea what, though the words to describe what happened poked through over the years in my journals.) I had tried to share words from my journal with the traditional therapist in Wellfleet, but nothing took root. She was not conscious enough to guide me.

Now, when I said "something happened", even though I sensed what the "something" was, like I would pick the correct answer on a multiple choice test if given the opportunity, still, I could not stand behind the words as I could stand behind the statement, "I know this pencil will fall to the ground when I drop it." My words had no gravity because I had not yet connected to the past experience to which they pointed.

Eagle Message: "Tell the Truth"

I wanted to see the eagles at the dog park. None were there. Wonderful silence and play with Horton though. On the way home, I decided to drive into City Park to look again for an eagle. We walked along the river where they usually sit high in the trees, but none were there. Then, on the way out of the park, I spotted one sitting in the top of the pin oak tree just behind the outer pond. I park. Horton and I walk towards him. We're about a hundred feet away. I say, "Tell me what to write today, where to go with the book?"

He says, "Tell the truth" — then flies away toward the river.

My Eleven-Year-Old Self

After a few sessions, Betsy guided me to connect to my eleven-year-old self. I saw clearly the orange bedspread, Dad, my younger self. I saw the desk where we wrote the essay and the mirror above the desk. I also felt my younger self and thereby opened a connection to her so that she was not absent from me anymore, or I from her. We dialogued:

You're not going to believe me are you? she said.

I do. I do believe you.

It was my fault wasn't it?

Sweetheart no, it was not your fault.

But Daddy loves me.

He does. Part of him made a mistake. It was wrong for him to touch you in the way he did.

Does it make me bad?

No! What he did has nothing to do with you, sweetheart. He made a big mistake. What matters now is that I help you to feel who you really are. What matters now is that you and I bond in our hearts and I love you so much that you can feel my love. There are things you decided about yourself, about other people, and about the world because of the incident that I will help you realize are not true. It will be a journey the two of us take. Does this make sense to you, Little Nancy?

Yes, but I feel like crying now.

I'll hold you and you can cry and cry as long as you need to. Let it all out. I am here for you now. You are so beautiful and wise and filled with love and true passion. You see, even though you decided that there was something wrong with your body, your sexuality, your very Self, there is not. Even though you decided that when you succeed in the world, something bad will happen too, that is not true.

I am here to teach you and support you to realize in the deepest cells of your body that you are perfect, whole, and just as Spirit made you. In fact, we are Spirit expressing as Nancy!

Amnesia: The Best Choice at the Time

I dissociated from my body and the experience of my father and me. I forgot the incident, how his arms spoke, where his hands moved that suddenly seemed, well, normal. I say normal because when a child's dependency is deep (and it always is), whatever shape love takes seems acceptable.

But, in my case, acceptance of this kind required amnesia. I could not consciously remember any 'incident'. I loved my dad. I needed him. After Mom died, I feared his death too. In the evening watching television, he would fall asleep on the couch. I'd stare at his shirt to make sure it was moving, to make sure he was breathing. He used to pause between breaths. I remember those pauses. Sometimes adrenalin would shoot into my bloodstream during those pauses because I thought he had died. Yes, my dependency was deep.

The eleven-year-old part of me who experienced Dad's violation of me went below the surface. And she, who endured so much that day, because she dissociated perfectly, allowed me to continue to love my father as if nothing (for there *was* nothing in my conscious mind) had happened. (And nothing ever did happen after that incident.) She who held the experience I could not consciously hold, paved the way for me to move forward in love, seeing the good, hoping for inspiration, for a moment when suddenly I would be whole again, like I was when the milkman asked me what I wanted to be when I grew up. There were no shadows covering my Light then.

And that moment came. Not just once, but many times, for the path of healing, transformation and the evolution of consciousness is never-ending. It is filled with many moments of Light, Love and awakening as we stay present, here, now, and remember to feel and listen to any aspect of our Self that needs to be heard and understood, that needs to be brought into this moment.

Drumming, the Loud Voice, and the God of Thunder

1998

Thunder circles our house. Horton stays close, stares at me for reassurance. The whites of his eyes beg for understanding. I tell him everything's okay. We wait for the lightning to flash again. He crawls under my desk, puts his big black head on my red Polartec slippers. I do nothing but watch and listen to the storm. The Loud Voice inside my head, the voice of the conditioned mind, the voice that formed to protect me at age eleven, takes this opportunity of stillness to accuse me of laziness, not enough productivity, not enough income. She says, "What you write here is all a lie."

I take a deep breath.

I ask the God of Thunder to speak to her, to illuminate the qualities of life apart from what one produces or earns. To tell her that my writing is not a lie.

I should have asked the God of Thunder to tell me what to tell her. It is *my* job to speak to her, *my* job to receive Guidance and speak it to the Loud Voice. My job. No one else can do this. No one else can know our weak places in consciousness or mend them with Love and Truth. They may be able to help us see the weak places, the places rampant with false beliefs and memories of the past, but no one else can actually do the healing, the reorientation to alignment with Self, with Source.

This is an important aspect of healing. To heal is to release illusions we have embraced as truth.

The Loud Voice is the part of me who created false beliefs about myself, who saw me through the eyes of Dad and Sally, rather than through the eyes of Spirit. The Loud Voice had to somehow make sense of what happened and so decided I was bad. The flaws I thought they saw in me I decided were true. The feeling of powerlessness I felt within the family I decided was the real me. This is the part that decided those things. It is also called the false self. This false self always gets created, no matter what the circumstances. It entraps our Essence through patterns of habituated thoughts and feelings. It's the shadow blocking out our Light. Though it is not real, in the sense of "You can't turn on a dark switch," it is real in the sense of the psychological experience of our human form.

It's my job now to teach this false self, to love her from a place of greater awareness. However, on this day, because of her intensity, I deferred to the God of Thunder. I felt scared of her.

Hail the size of mothballs pounds the kitchen greenhouse window. The maidenhair fern trembles. The God of Thunder tells me to drum and tells the Loud Voice to listen to the drumming. I follow this Guidance, reach for my Remo drum hanging on the wall beside me. I stand up, hold the drum in place, and stare through the window to the birch forest in the distance.

My rhythm starts slowly. Soon, I am chanting sounds of a language no longer spoken. My mouth does what it wants, independent of my mind. My throat expands and feels ancient to me. These sounds exist somewhere beyond this rainy Saturday, as if just past the woods another reality beckons. And in that world my Loud Voice can't take hold and shake me with her judgment. She doesn't need to. She no longer berates me. She can't scare me in that world where the drumming takes me because that world is filled with nothing but Love.

After the drumming ends, and after the rain stops, my Loud Voice wants to know if I love her. She says, "Why do you try to make me go away if you love me?" I call on the God of Thunder but he has left. I hang the drum in its place. I fix a cup of green tea. Horton has fallen asleep on his new bed in the living room.

"I love you," I say, staring at the little stuffed leopard, which represents the Loud Voice part of me. "I love you because you are part of me. I love you because you took on the false beliefs only to protect me. I understand this. It's okay now, though. We can let those go." I feel her accept my love and she cries. It's the cry of heartbreak. Her heart was broken. I let her cry to heal our heartbreak, for it broke the heart of my younger self to believe that she was flawed in such deep ways. There is suddenly peace, wholeness, and an emergence of Presence from beneath the hard thoughts embedded in my psyche for decades.

I walk outside to breathe fresh air. I look toward the back of the yard at the wire fence, scan the woods, the beautiful birch trees.

I focus. Suddenly, I see the large face of a black bear staring back at me. Our eyes meet.

How the Story Creates Reality

2009

Right now, the rain stopped. Right now, Horton rests at my feet. Right now, the water boils. Right now, my greatest desire is to write about how the story in my head creates my experience of life. Yet, there is so much to say about this subject that my tendency is to simply get up and do something other than allow words to flow.

Einstein said that the most important question to ask is whether we believe we live in a benevolent universe or a hostile one. My favorite way to approach this question is to bring it into daily life, into the moment.

Being conscious means to be aware of the story going on in our head, to be aware of our thoughts, beliefs and feelings right now. Yes, it would be wonderful not to have a story at all, perhaps, but stopping the narrative requires practice, not to mention mastery. Besides, it's the unconscious story that wreaks havoc, that blocks our Essence from shining. If we don't make it conscious, it wins. The next best thing to being totally free of the story is to be conscious of it; then we can start to see how the story is, indeed, creating our experience of life. Then, we can inquire about it.

My earlier reference to my 'tendency' to get up when I feel that there is 'so much to say' is an example of a story. It's a conditioned one, from very early in my life.

The self-concept this story hangs onto goes something like "My perceptions are crazy" "I can't write about these topics because I'm not qualified." I no longer abide by such a story or such a belief; however, as I evolve I find that remnants of early programming do indeed surface from time to time.

Pesky old beliefs.

The Little Choices

I'm learning to practice a greater awareness of focus. Where is my attention now? Is this where I want my attention to be? Reality exists only where the mind creates a focus. What we focus on expands. When the rain comes down hard and the gray sky feels oppressive, I tend to get distracted; I think about the sun. I take extra vitamin D3. I may say, "I need some tacos." Today, however, because I'm preparing for a detox diet, I'm trying to avoid the tacos and any processed food, though I had a couple crackers.

16.

My Last Visit with Dad

2007

When I opened the door to the nursing home, I focused on the shiny floors rather than death. Horton walked by my side. His tall black Lab stature drew attention from everyone, the nurses patted his head and the white-haired, sleepy people slumped over in their wheelchairs lining the hallway looked up in slow motion; a couple of them whispered, "A dog."

As I anticipated this visit, I feared that Dad would not recognize me. Although being recognized, or being seen, occurs on many levels, and my history of being seen by him lacked depth, I still wanted to feel connected to him, at least mentally. If he had become one of those very old people who could not bring forth their conscious mind through communication, I wasn't sure what I would do.

He was sitting with his head down in a wheelchair in his private room facing the television. I walked around him so that I could face him. I sat on his bed. "Dad, it's me, Nancy."

He lifted his head, opened his eyes. I reached across his eating table to turn off the television. I kept my body still so he could see me. I stared into his eyes. After a few moments, our eyes locked. "Hi Nancy," he smiled.

Then, there was silence, but we kept staring, facing each other. I thought how his face looked like the full moon, bright and spacious. It seemed translucent. How could he appear so clear when he was too weak to even lift his legs?

"You look so happy," he said. There was a slight lilt in his voice, a brief emergence of emotion. I felt his love then. "I am happy," I said, emphasizing the 'am'. We sat silently again. Kept our faces glued to each other's gaze.

When I was two, I walked from my sandbox to the hydrangea bush and cupped my hands around one large blossom, felt the round ornament of nature pulsating. Not long after being born, I learned to depend upon Nature for my sense of connection.

Now, our faces, Dad's and mine, seemed like round hydrangea blossoms, nodding in the breeze. We had never seen one another in this way before. Always, words clouded our spirit, his words overpowering me, or my words judging him.

He soon asked me to help him into bed and drifted into sleep.

I left him there and walked Horton outside the nursing home into the large grassy field at the end of the building. It was dusk. The killdeers flew around the edge of the field. Their familiar high-pitched mournful call touching my heart — *kill-dee, kill-dee*.

The mantra I learned at Kripalu suddenly came forth into my awareness, so I began to chant in a whisper as I walked: Om Namo Bagavate Vasudevaya. Horton and I walked around and around the field, listening to the killdeers, watching the sun fade away. And I chanted. I needed to quiet my mind, to be like the killdeers, completely focused on one moment, my shoe in the green grass, violet sky, and Horton by my side.

Dad died six months after this visit.

What I Read at Dad's Funeral

I loved my father. I loved him for his suffering of my mother's death. I loved him for his sense of humor. He would say to the women customers with curlers in their hair, "How many stations do you get with those?" He would say to customers with too much perfume on, "Doesn't that stuff get in your eyes?" I loved him for his hard work. I loved him for his generosity, for his service to the community. Many times he called our U.S. Congressman's office to expedite local people getting food stamps. I loved him for his love of Nature. For teaching me to canoe, to garden. I loved him for his sweet corn, for the corn roasts with friends. I loved him for buying fireworks and having parties and making sure everything was safe for me. I loved him for building his dream house for Mom, Sally and me to live in. I loved him for his stories about his childhood, about the village, about his father and his mother. I loved him for his love of democracy, for the party he had when Kennedy won. I loved him for giving speeches to organizations. I loved him for singing solos at church. I loved him for teaching Sunday School yet admitting he wasn't certain about God, though he was certain about Jesus and his goodness. I loved him for having a grocery store, for teaching me about business, for letting me work there. I loved him for his conversations in the store. I loved him for feeding me good food. I loved him for being an environmentalist before it was a movement, for making the deliverymen turn off their trucks before bringing in the goods. I loved him for not allowing the state to spray DDT on our woods when it was still legal to do that. I loved him for being kind to neighbors. I loved him for teaching me how to plant tomatoes. I loved him for visiting me at the yoga center. I loved him for being active in his life. I loved him for living to ninety-eight. I loved him for doing community theatre until he was ninety-three. I loved him for teaching me how to fish. I loved him for letting me go away to work the summer I was sixteen. I loved him for being a Democrat. I loved him for telling me how much he loved my mother. I loved him for his love of great acting. I loved him for his lack of complaint. I loved him for his self-discipline. I loved him for his valuing of pure spring water. I loved him for his resilience. I loved him for asking me every time we talked, "Are you happy?" I loved him for arguing with me. I loved him for holding my hand at Mom's funeral. I loved him for being against the Vietnam War. I loved him for teaching me how to catch minnows. I loved him for teaching me how to cut meat. I loved him for our canoe ride down New Creek when the water was flood level. I loved him for loving my cats. I loved him for the trips to Mom's grave every Memorial Day; for trimming the grass around all the gravestones; for letting me pick the peonies. I loved him for washing the gravestones. I loved him for telling me about each person there. I loved him for buying me a new Volkswagen Beetle in 1965. I loved him for not being angry when I had my first and only car wreck. I loved him for teaching me to drive defensively. I loved him for writing me letters. I loved him for loving my dog. I loved him for not being bitter about the nursing home. I loved him for seeing the good. I loved him for seeing the good.

Finish the Book

2010

It rained hard last night, so hard that today water stands in the fields, making little puddles beside the dried stubble of last season's corn stalks. As we walk the trail, Horton and I come upon a killdeer flying high over the field with slow, deep wingbeats, giving its *kill-dee, kill-dee* call repeatedly.

"Hi Dad," I say. Horton and I stop walking. He eats some tall green grass along the fence line. The wind whips my face. My nose runs. No one is around but us. The trail is not heavily traveled, but on sunny days, I generally run into a few people.

I listen. I want to hear the Guidance I know is there for me, in this moment, a repeated moment with the killdeer, a bird I first learned about as a child with Dad, who taught me about birds because he lived with an active relationship to Nature. When the killdeers made a nest in the middle of our gravel driveway, he would instruct the family to be careful as we drove up the hill.

"What?" I ask the killdeer posing as my father, or my father posing as the bird, it doesn't really matter to me, these intricacies of Spirit in my life.

The tricky part of hearing this sort of guidance is that my ego doesn't want to hear. So as I listen, it's as if I have to tilt my head like a bird, readjust my inner focus so that I can translate the squawking and squealing of my beloved bird, whose very skinny legs I've always felt such love for. At first, the message is a blur, to my outer ears practically inaudible. My inner ears, however, hear the message loud and clear. "Finish the book!" he says.

Afterward

I dream I am with Barack and Michelle. Barack and I are standing together and he is taking notes from something I am sharing with him. Then, I walk across the room and sit on the couch beside Michelle. She looks over at me and asks, "Why haven't I heard about you?" I reply, "Because I don't stand behind my work."

I dreamed this dream as a reminder about the importance of standing behind my work. Without this, no one else can benefit from whatever gifts I express. Standing behind one's work is, in many ways, harder than creating the work in the first place.

This dream reminded me that standing behind my work, that being visible in the world, that claiming my wisdom, my innate authority, and my Light is the most important thing there is to do. Not just for me, but for everyone.

We are here to bring forth the fullness of our Spirit.

We *are* consciousness. The stories, the pain and the perceived limitations are all there so that we can realize we are not that. We need the contrast in order to see. We need the wound in order to realize it is not the whole truth.

Life wakes us up when we want to awaken. Every moment, experience, pain, fear, joy, and encounter — all of it we project onto the screen of our life. Then we get to see it. Choose it or not. Imagine something else. Become something else. We get to keep waking up into a greater reality of who we can be. The greatest of course is Love.

Acknowledgments

This book has had a long gestation time. I have many people to thank. Without you, there would be no book.

To those who have been with me from the beginning — Zoe Jilleen, Rasmani Deborah Orth, and Eileen Donovan — thank you for your deep listening, for believing in my writing. You are my soul sisters and our hearts are always connected.

I want to thank my friends Joanne and David for letting me take up residence in their beautiful Nags Head apartment for a six-week writing retreat where I brought this book to its first completion and escaped an Iowa winter taboot!

Thank you, my dear friend Judith Stitzel, for our long and profound journey together. When I was a young woman in your class I had no idea this moment would come. Thank you for everything you are and have always been. Your support during this final period of completion and publication has been invaluable and has touched me deeply.

Special thanks to an old friend, Hank Trout. Our graduate school friendship got renewed when I asked him to read the first version of the finished manuscript. Your feedback and support meant so much to me.

Thank you Stephanie Catlett for being the genius editor that you are. Our weekend in Charlotte, with you at the helm, slicing and dicing the finished manuscript, is a weekend etched in my memory under the heading: best all time weekends ever! I came to you with 40,000 words and I left with a book. You are phenomenal.

And thank you Lois Rose, my second editor and proofreader. Knowing that you 'got' my book made me know I was in safe hands. This book would not be what it is without you. Your feedback on the tiniest things was brilliant and I can't wait to meet you in France for that walk on the hill.

Lynne Klippel: thanks for your guidance as we 'cut the cord' in the birthing of my book. Your publishing and marketing expertise brought this book to the world — literally. You taught me another level of trust.

I am grateful to Vermont College of Fine Arts for their outstanding creative nonfiction program and for my teachers there, especially Ellen Lesser and Phillip Graham.

Thank you Susanna McCan, my new friend and mastermind buddy extraordinaire. Our soul connection along with your solid feminine wisdom has made it so much easier to balance running my business and publishing a book all at the same time.

Finally, I want to thank my most important mentors and teachers: Dr. Margaret Paul, Robert Brumet, Carol Lampman, Eckhart Tolle, Esther Hicks and Abraham, John Randolph Price, and Neville Goddard. It really is true that we cannot be ourselves without each other.

About the Author

 A Transformational Coach and Spiritual Mentor, Nancy has been supporting women and men to heal, transform, and evolve in consciousness for over twenty years. In the newest iteration of her business, she serves both emerging and established women leaders through her transformational coaching program *Find Your Voice | Stand Behind It | Change the World.*

Nancy is a certified facilitator of the acclaimed Inner Bonding® spiritual healing process. She has traveled to London each year since 2011 to lead the Inner Bonding® weekend workshop. While in England, she also teaches workshops on self-love, consciousness, and writing.

Quite serendipitously, she began to paint in 2010. Having no formal art training, she was encouraged by a local gallery owner and artist to paint from her heart. She has received much praise for her work and her innate knowledge of color. Her paintings hang on walls in over five countries and fifteen states. Her artist's statement and art can be viewed at http://artfiftytwo.com/nancy-swisher.

Nancy holds an MFA in Creative Nonfiction from Vermont College of Fine Arts. She was awarded the New York Individual Artists Grant for poetry in 1983 and has published prose and poetry in *Earth's Daughters, Iowa Woman, IKON, upstreet* and *The Berkshire Review.* Portions of this book received honorable mention at the Artists at Work Fellowship Competition and were a finalist for the Callum MacLeod Memorial Publishing Prize.

When she is not painting, writing, or working with clients, she enjoys walking in nature, photographing birds, and having soulful conversations with friends. She still lives in Iowa.

To learn more about Nancy's work go to
www.nancyswisher.com.

A Reader's Companion Resource Page

Now that you have experienced this book, I encourage you use the Resource page on my website to go deeper with your own journey of finding your voice and exploring your own awakening.

On this page you will find:

- A set of 20 inquiry questions to guide you toward your inner wisdom and the voice of your deepest Self. These are perfect for book groups.
- A self-discovery assessment tool on the subject of Find Your Voice | Stand Behind It | Change the World.
- A guided audio meditation for tapping into the Presence of love within you.
- A Facebook Study Group

Go to this link to access your Resource Page:
http://nancyswisher.com/bookresources